Meal Prep
on a Budget

Meal Prep on a Budget

* * * * * * * * * * * * * * * * * *

How to Prep Healthy Meals on $40 a Week

* * * * * * * * * * * * * * * * *

Matt Kearns

Photography by Darren Muir

ROCKRIDGE
PRESS

I dedicate this book to my lovely wife Heather.

Thank you for being my best friend.

Contents

Introduction

Finding time in the week to meal prep for yourself can be a difficult task. I get it. First, you must find some healthy recipes you like. Second, you need to organize those healthy recipes into a shopping list and hope that the ingredients fit into your weekly budget. Third, you must make time around your busy schedule to cook these meals and hopefully not take up an entire day of your time off. At this point it may just be easier to order a pizza and not worry about the rest of the week, right? Cooking can be a hassle, and it can feel easier and cheaper to get some takeout.

I am here to tell you that there is a better way. I am a professionally trained chef who has offered healthy meal prep options to everyone from busy families to professional athletes. I have over 15 years of experience in the culinary industry, but my passion and style are geared more toward simple, delicious meals that can be easily replicated and prepped. There's something about a refrigerator full of individually packed meals that gets me excited.

I created this meal prep cookbook for people just like you. You're tired of eating unhealthy takeout or overpriced meals and need a simple solution for tasty dishes that are good for you. They also need to be easy to create and fit your budget.

That's exactly what you will get out of this book. In the pages that follow, you will get access to many simple and delicious recipes that don't break the bank. These recipes will be easy to prepare with straightforward cooking methods that use everyday, affordable ingredients. I'm going to take my expertise from working in professional kitchens and simplify the process to help you hack your way to tasty meal prep on a budget.

I'm also going to give you many great ideas in this book on how to shop frugally. It's easy to over-spend on ingredients, thinking you're saving money. Or maybe you don't know the ins and outs of your local grocery store. In this book you'll find my secret tips and tricks on how to save a lot of money and also get a lot of value in your food.

I'm going to combine this knowledge into four weeks of easy-to-follow meal preps. Each prep will include detailed shopping lists, step-by-step cooking methods, and storage instructions that will change the way you think about meal prep. You'll become a rock star in the kitchen after I show you how easy it is to create a balanced weekly meal plan for $40 per week. One of the biggest misconceptions around healthy eating is that it must be expensive. There's a lot of marketing today telling you that organic is the only way to go, or that you should only eat fresh produce and not frozen.

This meal prep cookbook is going to change the way you think about eating. All your friends and co-workers are going to see your healthy meals and ask if you hired a professional chef! That's going to be my goal here: to give you insider knowledge on how to cook food simply and easily and stay on that $40 a week budget. Let's dive in!

Part One

Meal Prep Made Frugal

You're about to embark on a fun journey to make your life easier in the kitchen. Cooking healthy, affordable meals is going to become easy for you using the information in this book. In this part, I'll discuss meal prep basics and how to stock your kitchen for success, and I'll provide four full weeks of preps to get you started—each week costing $40 or less. Let's picture it now. You're rocking out to your favorite playlist in the kitchen on a Sunday. You're looking forward to the upcoming week because your refrigerator is full of healthy meals. You're feeling confident and content. This can be you every week!

CHAPTER ONE

Budget Meal Prepping 101

This first chapter is going to pave the way for your meal prep experience. Even though every meal prep experience is unique to the individual, I'm going to start off with some basic ideas about ways you can start to think about meal prepping frugally. I'll go over topics such as budgeting, seasonal ingredients, and how to meal prep for multiple people. This chapter will also teach you how to set up your kitchen. Hopefully you are getting excited. I know I am!

Why Meal Prep Fits the Bill

Human beings are busier than ever these days. Whether you are a full-time employee, a parent, are running your own business, or any combination of these, it feels as if there isn't enough time in the day to eat properly. Many times, the default option after a long day is kicking your feet up with some takeout or unhealthy convenience food. Even if you do get time to meal prep, you may end up buying whatever is on sale with no real plan for how to use it. You might even over-buy and then ingredients or whole meals end up in the trash, leaving you feeling frustrated.

What's nice about meal prep is that everything is planned ahead of time. It's easier to stick to healthy eating when you know that the refrigerator is packed full of tasty, portion-conscious meals that don't cost an arm and a leg.

The rest of this chapter will help you start working through the meal prep process. You'll learn everything from identifying a food budget, to how to store food properly so that the meals last for the entire week and still taste delicious.

Chapters 2 through 5 will give you a great start with four weeks' worth of meal preps that walk you through every step in the process. These chapters will help you for the first month but will also act as a guide that you can come back to when you are meal prepping on your own.

Healthy and Affordable?

Sometimes eating on a budget isn't perceived as healthy. This is because some convenience foods can be overly processed or contain unhealthy additives—not the most nutritious options. But there are plenty of ways to eat both healthily *and* with an eye toward cost. Here are a few:

PREPARING MEALS IN ADVANCE MAKES YOU MORE CONSCIOUS ABOUT PORTION SIZE. We get so used to seeing the sizes of fast food or restaurant meals that we forget what proper portion sizes look like. Meal prep takes out the guesswork.

NUTRIENT-DENSE FOODS MAKE YOU FEEL FULLER FOR LONGER. Eating three ounces of chicken, a half-cup of cooked rice, and sautéed veggies will satiate you better than a takeout cheeseburger and fries.

STICKING TO A MEAL ROUTINE PREVENTS DEVIATING AND EXTRA SNACKING.
Having a plan for meals and shopping lists will keep you on track and make you less likely to reach for the potato chips.

REACH FOR VEGETARIAN PROTEIN OPTIONS, WHICH ARE CHEAPER THAN ANIMAL PROTEINS. Adding cooked lentils to your meatloaf, for instance, will keep you full, and you'll spend less on the ground beef.

STICK TO WHOLE FOODS, WHICH ARE LESS EXPENSIVE THAN PROCESSED OPTIONS. Making a homemade potato gratin will be cheaper than buying the premade, processed option.

Identify Your Food Budget

There are a few important factors when deciding on your meal prep budget. How many people are you cooking for? What types of ingredients are seasonal in your area? Are there some wholesale options where you can purchase some dry goods cheaper that will last you the whole month? Should you include grocery shopping as well as eating out? Are you someone who requires more protein in your diet or have other considerations?

Once you have outlined what your budget needs are, then you can find the best way to track your expenses. There are many apps out there that can help you with this. One of my favorite hacks is to find a local grocery store that does online ordering. You can simply take the food prep list you have and enter it in and see what the total comes to. There's nothing worse than being at the grocery store without a plan, trying to purchase ingredients on a budget, only to find out at the register that you overspent.

Plan Your Meals

This is the most crucial part of the whole process—deciding what meals you are going to prepare for the week. It's important to identify dishes that work best for your personal tastes, as well as the meal prepping process. Here are some ideas to think about when deciding on your meal selections.

DETERMINE THE MEALS YOU WOULD LIKE TO PREPARE. This book offers dozens of recipes to inspire you on your meal prep journey. But you can also search online, through apps like Pinterest or even googling your favorite types of dishes.

DO THE RECIPES UTILIZE INGREDIENTS YOU ALREADY HAVE? It's easier to start with recipes that make use of ingredients you already have on hand. Building up a well-stocked pantry over time can make this process even easier.

BUY INGREDIENTS YOU CAN USE IN MULTIPLE DISHES. When shopping, keep an eye out for ingredients you can use in multiple recipes. For instance the egg bites and chicken scallopini recipes in week 1's meal prep (page 18) both utilize frozen cauliflower and broccoli. This simplifies the purchasing and prepping process.

CHOOSE MEALS THAT ARE IDEAL FOR PREP. Salads are a great, healthy option, but they tend not to hold up well in the refrigerator for more than a few days. Choose recipes that last longer in the refrigerator or that can be frozen and reheated when you need them.

Shop Smart

Planning out your meals in advance can make things easier when it comes to shopping and staying under budget. Here are some great examples of ways you can streamline the process of shopping and still be conscious of price.

SHOP ONLINE. We live in a time where you can shop for everything online. Grocery shopping has become even easier with the options to have staff pick the food items for you and deliver them to your door. Plus, online shopping gives you a chance to look at all the items you need to buy before you purchase. You can even compare two or more stores to see if one offers cheaper options.

SHOP SEASONAL. Buying ingredients that are in season usually offers a better price, higher quality, and more nutrient density. Also look at local seasonal options, as these items may not have travelled as far, which would also decrease the price.

BUY IN BULK . . . SOMETIMES. I usually only buy what I need for a week, but sometimes it's beneficial to buy more of some items when you know you will use them every week. I like to purchase items like rice and pasta in bulk because they are very shelf-stable, and you can buy large amounts inexpensively.

LOOK FOR GENERIC BRANDS. When looking for pantry staples, it's often best to look at the store's generic brand. Their offerings are almost always less expensive than the competition, and you get the same quality as the leading competitor.

LOOK FOR SALES AND BE FLEXIBLE. A recipe might call for chicken breasts, but perhaps the chicken thighs that are on sale will work just as well. Be open and flexible in the kitchen and always look for the best deals.

THINK SHRINKAGE. When buying protein, it's beneficial to look at fat content and protein content. When buying ground beef, I will often buy the leanest option because you will get a higher yield per price, because you lose yield when the fat cooks off.

ORGANIC MAY NOT ALWAYS WORK. It's tempting to look at organic options over conventional produce, but often you end up just spending more and the quality isn't much better. If budget is your top concern, reach for conventional produce.

Frozen Assets

Frozen items are going to be your best friend in meal prep. Using frozen ingredients has many benefits over fresh items because they last for months without spoiling, are often cheaper, and can sometimes be more nutritious. Here are a few examples of frozen items and great reasons to use them.

BERRIES/FRUIT. Say goodbye to rotting strawberries in your refrigerator! Using frozen fruit is often more nutritious than fresh because they're flash-frozen at their nutritional peak. They're also less expensive.

FROZEN VEGGIE MIXES. The veggies are already cut and mixed, so all you need to do is cook them! They work great in soups and stews, as well as stir-fries.

SPINACH. Spinach is another fresh ingredient that often goes bad quickly. Frozen spinach is a nutritional powerhouse that's great in eggs, lasagna, and smoothies, and a great way to get a serving of greens in a pinch.

FROZEN MEAT AND SEAFOOD. Frozen protein makes life much easier in the kitchen. No leaks from fresh protein in the refrigerator making a mess or contaminating other foods. And the cost is often more reasonable, too.

Prep, Prep, Prep

Once you have chosen your recipes, you need to plan a day to prepare everything. I usually recommend one to two prep days, to simplify things. If you happen to work a Monday through Friday job, then a weekend day, such as Sunday, may be the best day for you. If you are able to, it would also be good to look at a second day, like Wednesday (or halfway through your work week). Because most foods only last safely in the refrigerator for five days, some people take an extra day to prep for the last two days of the week. Or you might need an extra day if you're

meal prepping for more than just yourself. For instance, Sunday might be a perfect day to organize all your ingredients and recipes and cook the first half of the meals. Then on Wednesday, perhaps, you can prepare the second half of the week's meals. If this doesn't work for you, it's fine to cook and prepare everything in one day. All the meals in this book are easy and budget-friendly, so none of them take a ton of time or effort to make.

The meal preps included here will walk you through the whole process and give you a good head start in showing you how to prepare for future weeks. The meals in these plans are easy to prepare and designed to last for days in the refrigerator. You should also look at how to organize your preparation steps. Think about things like cook times, whether you need to defrost certain proteins, and starting with the more time-consuming recipes.

Store and Enjoy

An important part in meal prepping is storing the food in individual containers for the upcoming days of the week. One of the most necessary steps is to make sure to cool the food as best as you can before portioning in individual containers. If you portion food and put the lids on while hot, it can create extra moisture and the meals can spoil faster. Also keep in mind that if there are sauces or dressings in your meals, you'll probably want to keep them in separate containers, so food doesn't get soggy.

Each recipe in this book has specific storing procedures so you can get the most out of your meals. You may find the following chart useful as you start to meal prep your own recipes and need to know how long they will last in the refrigerator or freezer.

Food	Refrigerator	Freezer
Baked goods (muffins, breads)	5–7 days	1 month
Cooked poultry dishes	3–4 days	4–6 months
Cooked fish and seafood	3–4 days	4–6 months
Cooked meat dishes	3–4 days	2–3 months
Cooked vegetables	3–4 days	1 month
Hard-boiled eggs	1 week	Don't freeze
Heartier salads (pasta salad, potato salad)	3–5 days	Don't freeze
Leafy salads	3 days	Don't freeze
Prepared egg dishes	3–4 days	2–3 months
Soups and stews	3–4 days	2–3 months

Source: Food and Drug Administration Refrigerator and Freezer Storage Chart

The Frugal Kitchen

As nice as it seems to have the fanciest kitchen equipment, you won't need to purchase anything extravagant for the recipes found in this book because they require minimal cooking equipment to get the job done. The following items will make your meal prepping successful.

TOOLS AND EQUIPMENT

Here's a list of the equipment you will need to make all these tasty recipes:

- Chef's knife
- 1 large nonstick pan
- 1 (6-quart) pot with a lid
- 1 large baking sheet

- 12-cup muffin tin

- Cooking utensils: tongs, wooden spoons, spatula/scraper, whisk

- 1 small (2-quart) mixing bowl and 1 large (3-to-4-quart) mixing bowl

- Can opener

- Cutting board

- High-speed blender

- Meal prep containers (20): Choose a variety of sizes and make sure they are microwave- and dishwasher-safe and freezer-friendly

PANTRY STAPLES

The following list describes all the foods you will need to keep in your pantry to cook these recipes. I won't assume, however, that you have any of these items when calculating the weekly costs, except for the staples of olive oil, salt, and pepper.

- All-purpose flour

- Baking powder

- Balsamic vinegar

- Beef stock

- Chili powder

- Cinnamon, ground

- Curry powder

- Garlic powder

- Honey

- Hot sauce

- Italian seasoning

- Lentils, red

- Linguine

- Mayonnaise

- Parsley, dried

- Rice, medium-grain white

- Red pepper flakes

- Soy sauce

- Tomato sauce

- Vegetable stock

- Vinegar, red wine

Go-To Budget Meal Prep Meals

The goal here is frugality and simplicity, and it's beneficial for you, the cook, to learn how to prepare and master these items. As such, you'll see similar styles of dishes repeated throughout the book, as well as ingredients that can be maximized and reused. Repetition is actually a great thing—it sets you up for success, it allows you to perfect the things you love, and it makes it easier to introduce creativity slowly (e.g., trying a different spice blend) without burning out on difficulty or effort. An effective, successful professional kitchen works in a similar way, and it will work for you, too. Here are some common meals/items you will see in this book.

EGGS. One of my favorite staples and an inexpensive way to consume protein. There are many ways to cook eggs. You'll see them as frittatas, egg cups, poached eggs, and more.

GRAIN-BASED BOWLS. Grains and legumes like rice, lentils, and barley are a great and healthy way to fill up your stomach and still be mindful of costs.

GROUND MEATS. Many of the recipes in this book will use ground meat because it is a convenient, inexpensive option that is delicious when prepared properly.

ONE-PAN MEALS. This is one of my favorite meals because it's simple to put all your ingredients in one vessel, season, and cook! It also makes portioning and clean-up easy.

PASTAS. These are easy and can be healthy if you follow proper portioning. Adding vegetables and lean protein can make pasta a filling, nutritious option.

SMOOTHIES. Breakfast isn't complete without smoothies. You can add anything into a blender and in less than 30 seconds, you have a quick, nutritious breakfast.

SOUPS. Soup is one of the easiest meals to prepare on a budget and is a great way to use leftover ingredients and create filling meals you can reheat easily.

About the Meal Prep Plans

These meal preps are designed for one person. There will be five to six recipes per week that will yield enough food for 80 to 90 percent of your meals for the week. The other 10 percent of your meals might include eating a meal out or grabbing a previously frozen leftover meal.

$40 OR LESS PER WEEK

One of the main goals of this book is to show you how you can create thrifty, nutritious meals. Each week you will spend $40 or less on these meals. These costs include everything except for olive oil, salt, and pepper. The first week's shopping trip will prioritize the pantry staples that will be used in all four weeks. The USDA recommends $37 to $43 to feed yourself on a weekly frugal budget. This will be accomplished by using things like inexpensive proteins, frozen items, and reusing ingredients in several recipes. The meals will average $1 to $3 per serving. Costs of ingredients will vary by location and grocery store, so you may need to do a bit more research to get the best prices.

FEEDING MORE

When feeding more than one person using these meal preps, you will be able to double or triple the recipes when necessary. As I said earlier, you might want to add an extra prep day if cooking for more than just yourself.

A NOTE ON SNACKS

Although snacks aren't a part of the four weeks' worth of meal preps, I've included a chapter on frugal snack options that you can reference. Snacks can be inexpensive as well and, when made thoughtfully, can also offer as much nutritional value as a full meal. When preparing snacks, it may be beneficial to prepare them the day after your big meal prep day—a Monday, for example. This is a great way to use up leftovers and not get too burned out.

FLEXIBILITY IS YOUR FRIEND

Every recipe will offer tips that include suggestions on swapping out ingredients you might not have on hand. The recipes also list certain ingredients as optional if you need to be extra budget-conscious. The prep instructions will also be flexible, meaning you'll have the option of prepping all the meals in one day or splitting them into two days.

A NOTE ON SALT

You will notice that most of the recipes mention seasoning with salt and pepper to taste. Instead of including exact amounts of salt of pepper, here are some quick tips when seasoning your food:

- Add the seasoning gradually to build the flavor of your dishes.

- Check often throughout the cooking process by tasting your food and adjusting accordingly.

- Don't over-season too quickly; you can always add more salt, but you can't take it away!

Ground Pork
Stir-Fry, page 22

CHAPTER TWO

Week 1

Welcome to week 1 of your meal prep on a budget journey. I really like this first week because it utilizes a lot of ingredients in the same dishes. I use many frozen items here like broccoli and cauliflower, edamame, and stir-fry vegetables to make things easier. I am also a huge fan of eggs, and these egg bites will make life easier on busy mornings. You can even freeze them in larger batches, if you prefer. Let's begin.

Week 1

	Breakfast	Lunch	Dinner
Monday	Roasted Cauliflower and Broccoli Egg Bites (page 25)	Edamame Lentil Vegetable Soup (page 24)	Ground Pork Stir-Fry (page 22)
Tuesday	PB and J Smoothie (page 21)	Tuna Macaroni Salad (page 23)	Chicken Scallopini with Sautéed Green Beans (page 26)
Wednesday	Roasted Cauliflower and Broccoli Egg Bites	Edamame Lentil Vegetable Soup	Ground Pork Stir-Fry
Thursday	PB and J smoothie	Tuna Macaroni Salad	Chicken Scallopini with Sautéed Green Beans
Friday	Roasted Cauliflower and Broccoli Egg Bites	Edamame Lentil Vegetable Soup	Ground Pork Stir-Fry
Saturday	PB and J Smoothie	Tuna Macaroni Salad	Chicken Scallopini with Sautéed Green Beans
Sunday	Roasted Cauliflower and Broccoli Egg Bites	Edamame Lentil Vegetable Soup	Ground Pork Stir-Fry

Shopping List

PRODUCE

- Bananas (3)
- Cabbage, green (1 head)
- Carrots (2)
- Celery stalks (2)
- Cucumber (1)

- Garlic (1 bulb)
- Ginger (1-inch piece)
- Green beans (1 pound)
- Mushrooms, white button (8)
- Onions, small, white (2)

DAIRY AND EGGS

- Almond milk, unsweetened (4 cups)
- Eggs, large (12)

- Heavy whipping cream (½ cup)

MEAT AND SEAFOOD

- Chicken breast (about 10 ounces)

- Ground pork (1 pound)

FROZEN

- Broccoli and cauliflower mix (12 ounces)

- Edamame beans, shelled (12 ounces)
- Strawberries (8 ounces)

PANTRY

- Balsamic vinegar
- Black pepper, ground
- Dill, dried
- Dill pickles
- Flour, all-purpose
- Garlic powder
- Honey

- Hot sauce (optional)
- Italian seasoning
- Macaroni pasta (⅓ pound)
- Mayonnaise
- Olive oil
- Peanut butter
- Red lentils (½ cup)

- Red pepper flakes
- Salt
- Soy sauce

- Vegetable stock (4 cups)
- White rice, medium-grain
- White tuna (1 [5-ounce] can)

Prep It

1. Prep the smoothie portions for the PB and J Smoothies (page 21) and cut all the vegetables for all meals.

2. Cook the rice for the Ground Pork Stir-Fry (page 22), and cook the macaroni for the Tuna Macaroni Salad (page 23).

3. Prepare the Edamame Lentil Vegetable Soup (page 24) in its entirety.

4. Prepare the Roasted Cauliflower and Broccoli Egg Bites (page 25) and put them in the oven.

5. Make the Ground Pork Stir-Fry in its entirety.

6. Make the Chicken Scallopini with Sautéed Green Beans (page 26) in its entirety.

ADDITIONAL OR MID-WEEK PREP

1. You can bread and freeze half of the scallopini portions and eat them mid-week, if you'd like.

2. You can freeze half the egg bites and pull them out mid-week, as well.

3. Let everything cool before you package into containers.

PB and J Smoothie

Makes 3 smoothies | Prep Time: 2 minutes

$1.50 PER PORTION

In the world of meal prep nothing is easier and simpler than a smoothie. Throw in a cup of frozen ingredients, add some liquid, and you have a healthy breakfast in under two minutes. You don't even need an expensive blender. This simple smoothie tastes like a peanut butter and jelly sandwich! It uses frozen strawberries, peanut butter, almond milk, and a frozen banana to make things smooth and creamy.

3 bananas, sliced and divided
1½ cups fresh or frozen strawberries, divided

3 cups unsweetened almond milk
3 tablespoons smooth peanut butter
3 teaspoons honey

1. Into each of 3 resealable jars or containers, place 1 sliced banana and ½ cup of strawberries. Store in the freezer.
2. Into 3 separate containers, divide the almond milk, peanut butter, and honey. Store in the refrigerator.
3. On the day you'll be drinking it, add 1 portion of frozen fruit with 1 portion of the fresh ingredients to the blender. Blend until smooth.
4. You may need to add a bit of water to thin out the smoothie if it's too thick.

SMART SHOPPING: Many grocery stores offer peanut butter in the bulk section. They use a machine to crush the peanuts and oil so that it's free of other ingredients, and you only have to buy what you need.

Per serving (1 smoothie): Calories: 319; Fat: 11g; Protein: 11g; Carbohydrates: 51g; Fiber: 6g

Ground Pork Stir-Fry

Makes 4 servings | Prep Time: 15 minutes | Cook Time: 30 minutes

I love cooking with pork. It's a versatile protein that is easy to pair with many ingredients. This stir-fry is also a great way to use up leftover vegetables. Ground pork is cost-effective and simple to prepare, especially in stir-fries. I use a combination of fresh and frozen vegetables here, along with a simple sauce.

1¼ cups water
1 cup medium-grain white rice
Salt
2 tablespoons olive oil
1 pound ground pork
2 cups frozen broccoli and cauliflower florets
2 cups shredded green cabbage

8 white button mushrooms, sliced
2 garlic cloves, thinly sliced
1 teaspoon grated ginger
2 tablespoons soy sauce
1 tablespoon hot sauce
1 tablespoon honey
Freshly ground black pepper

1. In a small pot, combine the water and rice over medium-high heat. Season with salt and bring to a gentle boil. Cover, reduce the heat to low, and cook for 20 to 25 minutes, until the water has evaporated and the rice is light and fluffy. Set aside.
2. In a large pan over medium heat, pour in the olive oil. Add the pork, making sure to break it up well.
3. Once the pork is about half browned, 3 to 4 minutes, add the broccoli-cauliflower, cabbage, mushrooms, garlic, and ginger. Cook for 4 to 5 minutes, until the vegetables brighten in color.
4. Add the soy sauce, hot sauce, and honey and simmer for 1 to 2 minutes, mixing well.
5. Portion the meat and veggies evenly in 4 airtight containers with rice and cool. Store in the refrigerator for 4 to 5 days or freeze for 1 month.

SMART SHOPPING: Ground pork is a great inexpensive protein source that is readily available at most grocery stores.

Per serving: Calories: 431; Fat: 12g; Protein: 31g; Carbohydrates: 51g; Fiber: 4g

Tuna Macaroni Salad

Makes 3 servings | Prep Time: 10 minutes | Cook Time: 10 minutes

$1.70 PER PORTION

Canned tuna is a great, affordable source of protein. It's convenient to stock a few cans of this tasty fish in your pantry when you're craving a quick lunch. This filling salad also uses macaroni, fresh-cut vegetables, and a simple and tasty dressing. It's great any night of the week and could easily be turned into a casserole-type dish by melting some cheese on top.

1 cup macaroni noodles
1 (5-ounce) can flaked white tuna, drained
3 dill pickles, finely diced
½ cup shredded carrot
½ cup finely diced cucumber
½ cup finely diced celery

1½ tablespoons mayonnaise
1 tablespoon balsamic vinegar
1 teaspoon garlic powder
1 teaspoon hot sauce (optional)
1 teaspoon olive oil
Salt
Freshly ground black pepper

1. Bring a large pot of water to boil over high heat and cook the macaroni according to package directions. Make sure to stir while cooking because macaroni tends to stick.
2. Once cooked, drain the macaroni, run under cold water to cool, and transfer to a large bowl.
3. Add the tuna, pickles, carrots, cucumber, and celery. Mix well.
4. In a separate, medium bowl, whisk together the mayonnaise, vinegar, garlic powder, hot sauce (if using), and olive oil to make the dressing.
5. Add the dressing to the bowl with the tuna salad and mix well. Season with salt and pepper.
6. Portion evenly in 3 airtight containers. Store in the refrigerator for 4 to 5 days or freeze for up to 1 month.

SMART SHOPPING: Feel free to use another type of pasta, if you wish. Rigatoni or fusilli also work well here.

Per serving: Calories: 276; Fat: 9g; Protein: 15g; Carbohydrates: 34g; Fiber: 4g

Edamame Lentil Vegetable Soup

Makes 4 servings | Prep Time: 15 minutes | Cook Time: 30 minutes

I am a big fan of edamame as a high-protein, vegetarian option. It's also great because it comes frozen, and it's inexpensive as well, making it a fantastic option for meal prepping on a budget. This delicious soup uses both frozen and fresh vegetables and is perfect to make and freeze in larger batches.

2 tablespoons olive oil
1½ cups frozen shelled edamame
1 cup frozen broccoli and
 cauliflower florets
1 cup shredded green cabbage
1 celery stalk, diced
1 carrot, peeled and diced
¼ white onion, diced

1 teaspoon dried dill
1 teaspoon garlic powder
1 teaspoon red pepper flakes
4 cups vegetable stock
1 teaspoon soy sauce
¾ cup dry red lentils
Salt
Freshly ground black pepper

1. In a large pot over medium-high heat, pour in the olive oil. Add the edamame, broccoli and cauliflower mix, cabbage, celery, carrots, and onion and cook for 3 to 5 minutes, until the vegetables get just a bit of color in them.
2. Add the dill, garlic powder, and red pepper flakes and cook for another 1 to 2 minutes.
3. Pour in the vegetable stock and soy sauce and bring to a gentle simmer.
4. Once simmering, add the lentils and cook for 15 to 20 minutes. The lentils should be tender and not mushy. Season with salt and pepper after the soup comes to a simmer, because the reduced liquid will result in a saltier soup. Because of the soy sauce, you shouldn't need much seasoning here.
5. Transfer into 4 airtight containers. Store in the refrigerator for 4 to 5 days or freeze for 1 month.

SMART SHOPPING: I used the broccoli and cauliflower medley again, but feel free to use other vegetables.

Per serving: Calories: 286; Fat: 11g; Protein: 16g; Carbohydrates: 34g; Fiber: 9g

Roasted Cauliflower and Broccoli Egg Bites

. . . .

Makes 8 egg bites | Prep Time: 10 minutes | Cook Time: 15 minutes

Egg bites are one of my favorite meals to cook for breakfast. They are protein-packed, and you can add any vegetables you choose. In this recipe I use white onion with frozen broccoli and cauliflower. The broccoli and cauliflower are usually sold in the same package. The key to making this dish work is to pre-sauté the vegetables to develop flavor but also evaporate some of the water so the egg bites aren't too soggy.

1 tablespoon olive oil, plus more for greasing
⅔ cup frozen broccoli and cauliflower florets
2 tablespoons diced white onion

Salt
Freshly ground black pepper
½ teaspoon garlic powder
12 large eggs, beaten
½ teaspoon red pepper flakes

1. Preheat the oven to 385°F.
2. In a large sauté pan or skillet over medium heat, pour 1 tablespoon of olive oil. Add the broccoli and cauliflower and onion, and sauté for 2 to 3 minutes until the vegetables start to get some color. Season with salt, pepper, and garlic powder.
3. Grease 8 cups of a muffin tin with olive oil and portion the veggies evenly into the cups.
4. In a large bowl, season the egg mixture with salt, pepper, and red pepper flakes and pour evenly into the cups.
5. Bake for 10 to 12 minutes. Use a toothpick to check the center of the egg bites; the toothpick will come out clean when it's done. The eggs should have some color on top and be just cooked in the middle. Let cool and transfer to airtight containers. Store in the refrigerator for 4 to 5 days or freeze for up to 1 month.

SMART SHOPPING: Look for the larger packages of 18 or more eggs because they last for 2 to 3 weeks and are cheaper.

Per serving (2 egg bites): Calories: 253; Fat: 18g; Protein: 19g; Carbohydrates: 3g; Fiber: 1g

Chicken Scallopini with Sautéed Green Beans

· ·

Makes 3 servings | Prep Time: 10 minutes | Cook Time: 15 minutes

Chicken scallopini is a simple and delicious way of cooking chicken breasts. It takes only 3 to 4 minutes per side to brown the thinly sliced chicken and cook it through. This scallopini is paired with simple green beans cooked with a bit of olive oil and finished with a garlic cream sauce.

½ cup all-purpose flour
2 teaspoons garlic powder, divided
1 teaspoon Italian seasoning
⅔ pound boneless, skinless chicken breasts, halved horizontally to make thinner

Salt
Freshly ground black pepper
1 tablespoon olive oil
¼ cup finely diced white onion
1 pound green beans, trimmed
½ cup heavy whipping cream

1. In a shallow dish, mix the flour, 1 teaspoon of garlic powder, and the Italian seasoning. Season the breast halves with salt and pepper and dredge in the flour mixture well.

2. In a large pan over medium-high heat, pour in the olive oil, and cook the chicken breasts for 3 to 4 minutes per side, until browned and cooked through. Remove the chicken from the pan and set aside.

3. Add the onion and the remaining 1 teaspoon of garlic powder to the pan and sauté for 3 to 4 minutes, until softened. Add the green beans and cook for another 3 minutes, until the beans have some color in them.

4. Add the cream and cook until it's reduced by half, about 3 minutes. The sauce should coat the back of a spoon. Season with more salt and pepper, if needed.

5. Portion the chicken and green beans into 3 airtight containers and drizzle the sauce over top. Store in the refrigerator for 4 to 5 days or freeze for up to 1 month.

SMART SHOPPING: Look for deals at your grocery store on chicken breasts; they often come in a value pack for a great price. Chicken thighs can work for this dish, too.

Per serving: Calories: 422; Fat: 21g; Protein: 29g; Carbohydrates: 30g; Fiber: 5g

Mushroom and Zucchini Frittata, page 36

CHAPTER THREE

Week 2

This week you are in for a real treat. Some things that make it extra budget-friendly are the use of eggs in both breakfast and lunch, and also utilizing many frozen vegetables. There are lots of tasty flavors this week, from curry soup to beef and mushroom burgers.

Week 2

	Breakfast	Lunch	Dinner
Monday	Mushroom and Zucchini Frittata (page 36)	Tofu Curry Vegetable Soup (page 35)	Greek Chicken Rice Bowls (page 33)
Tuesday	Oatmeal with Stewed Fruit (page 37)	Egg Fried Rice with Edamame (page 34)	Deconstructed Beef and Mushroom Burger (page 38)
Wednesday	Mushroom and Zucchini Frittata	Tofu Curry Vegetable Soup	Greek Chicken Rice Bowls
Thursday	Oatmeal with Stewed Fruit	Egg Fried Rice with Edamame	Deconstructed Beef and Mushroom Burger
Friday	Mushroom and Zucchini Frittata	Tofu Curry Vegetable Soup	Greek Chicken Rice Bowls
Saturday	Oatmeal with Stewed Fruit	Egg Fried Rice with Edamame	Deconstructed Beef and Mushroom Burger
Sunday	Mushroom and Zucchini Frittata	Tofu Curry Vegetable Soup	Greek Chicken Rice Bowls

Shopping List

PRODUCE

- English cucumber, long (1)
- Garlic (5 cloves)
- Ginger (1-inch piece)
- Lemon (1)
- Mushrooms, white button (22)
- Red onion, small (1)
- Roma tomatoes (8)
- Scallions (1 bunch)
- White onions, small (2)
- Yam or sweet potato, medium (10 ounces)
- Zucchini (2)

DAIRY AND EGGS

- Butter (2 tablespoons)
- Eggs, large (18)
- Sour cream (1 cup)

MEAT, MEAT ALTERNATIVES, AND SEAFOOD

- Chicken breasts (1 pound)
- Firm tofu (12 ounces)
- Ground beef, lean (12 ounces)

FROZEN

- Berry medley (12 ounces)
- Broccoli and cauliflower medley (12 ounces)
- Edamame beans (4 ounces)
- Peas and carrots medley (4 ounces)
- Vegetable medley of choice (12 ounces)

PANTRY

- Black pepper, ground
- Chili powder
- Cinnamon, ground
- Curry powder
- Garlic powder
- Honey
- Italian seasoning
- Oats, quick (1½ cups)
- Olive oil
- Parsley

- Red pepper flakes
- Rice, white, medium-grain (12 ounces)
- Salt
- Soy sauce
- Sunflower seeds, shelled (4 ounces)
- Vegetable stock (4 cups)

Prep It

1. Cook the rice for the Greek Chicken Rice Bowls (page 33) and the Egg Fried Rice with Edamame (page 34).

2. Cut the vegetables for all the recipes while the rice cooks.

3. Prepare the Tofu Curry Vegetable Soup (page 35).

4. Cook the Mushroom and Zucchini Frittatas (page 36) and assemble the Oatmeal with Stewed Fruit (page 37) as the frittata cooks.

5. Prepare the Egg Fried Rice and the Deconstructed Beef and Mushroom Burgers (page 38).

6. Assemble the Greek Chicken Rice Bowls.

ADDITIONAL OR MID-WEEK PREP

1. The frittatas can be split up into two prep days.

2. The soup can be prepared and the portions frozen and then pulled out when you are ready to serve them.

Greek Chicken Rice Bowls

Makes 4 servings | Prep Time: 15 minutes | Cook Time: 30 minutes

These Greek chicken bowls are inexpensive and very easy to make. You can use chicken thighs or breasts—whatever's cheaper. Opting out of the feta cheese and olives in the salad cuts down on cost, and the sour cream adds flavor and creaminess.

1½ cups water
¾ cup medium-grain white rice
Salt
2 tablespoons olive oil, divided
1 pound boneless, skinless chicken thighs or breasts, cut into 1-inch strips
1 cucumber, seeded and diced into ¾-inch pieces

4 Roma tomatoes, diced into ¾-inch pieces
¼ cup red onion, diced into ¼-inch pieces
Juice of 1 lemon
1 tablespoon Italian seasoning
Freshly ground black pepper
4 tablespoons sour cream
1 teaspoon garlic powder

1. In a medium pot, combine the water and rice and lightly salt. Bring to a simmer over medium heat. Reduce the heat to low, cover, and cook for 25 minutes until all the moisture has evaporated and the rice is light and fluffy. Let cool.
2. In a large pan over medium-high heat, pour in 1 tablespoon of olive oil. Add the sliced chicken and cook until just cooked through and lightly browned, 4 to 5 minutes. Set aside.
3. In a large bowl, combine the cucumber, tomatoes, onion, the remaining 1 tablespoon of olive oil, lemon juice, and Italian seasoning. Season with salt and pepper.
4. In a separate small bowl, whisk together the sour cream and garlic powder and set aside.
5. Portion the salad, rice, and chicken into 4 airtight containers and top with the garlic sour cream dressing. Store in the refrigerator for 4 to 5 days or freeze for 1 month.

SMART SHOPPING: Typically this recipe would use oregano and basil, not Italian seasoning. But I use Italian seasoning in so many recipes that it's more cost-effective.

Per serving: Calories: 393; Fat: 14g; Protein: 27g; Carbohydrates: 39g; Fiber: 3g

Egg Fried Rice with Edamame

. . . .

Makes 3 servings | Prep Time: 10 minutes | Cook Time: 25 minutes

Fried rice is a Chinese staple that takes day-old rice and mixes it with scrambled eggs, vegetables, fresh garlic and ginger, and soy sauce. This version uses frozen veggies and edamame, as well as freshly sliced scallions and lots of garlic and ginger. I've made this dish for my son and he really enjoys it. It's an inexpensive and filling dish that can be made any night of the week.

1½ cups water
¾ cup medium-grain white rice
Salt
2 tablespoons olive oil
½ cup frozen shelled edamame, thawed
½ cup frozen peas and carrots, thawed
2 garlic cloves, chopped

1 teaspoon grated ginger
½ teaspoon red pepper flakes
6 large eggs, well beaten
2 teaspoons soy sauce
¼ cup sliced scallions, both green and
    white parts

1. In a medium pot, combine the water and rice. Season with salt and bring to a simmer over medium heat. Reduce the heat to low, cover, and cook for 25 minutes until all the moisture has evaporated and the rice is light and fluffy. Let cool.
2. In a large pan over medium-high heat, pour in the olive oil. Add the edamame, peas, and carrots and cook for 2 minutes.
3. Add the garlic, ginger, and red pepper flakes and cook for another 2 minutes until you can really smell the garlic and ginger.
4. Add the eggs and scramble well. Once the liquid from the egg has just disappeared, and the eggs are nice and fluffy, then add the rice and soy sauce.
5. Mix well and check for seasoning. Top with the scallions and portion into 3 airtight containers. Store in the refrigerator for 4 days or freeze for 1 month.

SMART SHOPPING: Edamame is a great source of protein and a cheap substitution for many types of protein.

Per serving: Calories: 450; Fat: 20g; Protein: 20g; Carbohydrates: 46g; Fiber: 3g

Tofu Curry Vegetable Soup

Makes 4 servings | Prep Time: 10 minutes | Cook Time: 25 minutes

This curry vegetable soup is one where you can add every frozen vegetable you have, and it'll always turn out delicious. The curry powder, garlic, and ginger flavor this soup, and you'll be surprised how easy it is to make. Plus, this soup is crazy inexpensive but is still healthy.

2 tablespoons olive oil
12 ounces firm tofu, cut into
    ½-inch pieces
2 cups frozen broccoli and
    cauliflower medley
2 cups frozen vegetables (such as car-
    rots, corn, peas, or green beans)
½ cup diced white onion

3 garlic cloves, chopped
2 teaspoons grated ginger
2 teaspoons curry powder
4 cups vegetable stock
½ cup water
Salt
Freshly ground black pepper

1. In a large pot over medium-high heat, combine the olive oil, tofu, broccoli and cauliflower, frozen vegetables, onion, garlic, and ginger and stir to combine.
2. Cook the vegetables for 5 to 6 minutes until some of the moisture has evaporated.
3. Add the curry powder and cook for 1 to 2 minutes.
4. Pour in the vegetable stock and water and bring to a simmer. Cook for 15 minutes and season with salt and pepper to taste.
5. Portion the soup into 4 airtight containers and let cool. Store in the refrigerator for 5 days or freeze for 1 month.

SMART SHOPPING: You can buy small amounts of raw ginger and keep it in a resealable bag in the freezer for up to 1 month. Grate the frozen ginger and you're good to go. You don't even need to peel it!

Per serving: Calories: 192; Fat: 11g; Protein: 12g; Carbohydrates: 16g; Fiber: 6g

Mushroom and Zucchini Frittata

Makes 6 servings | Prep Time: 10 minutes | Cook Time: 12 minutes

Frittatas are a nice and easy baked-egg dish that can be made in many ways. You can add any type of protein or vegetable you like. When I make frittatas, I often cook them with mushrooms, zucchini, and onions. I love the taste and textures that these vegetables impart. Using an oven-safe pan, simply sauté the veggies, add the eggs, and bake until lightly golden brown. Garnish with some fresh tomato, and you have a simple, satisfying dish that's cost-effective.

1 tablespoon olive oil
2 zucchini, finely diced
12 white button mushrooms, sliced
½ cup sliced white onion
2 teaspoons garlic powder
2 teaspoons Italian seasoning

Salt
Freshly ground black pepper
12 large eggs, well beaten
2 Roma tomatoes, finely diced,
    for garnish

1.   Preheat the oven to 400°F.
2.   In a large, oven-safe pan over medium-high heat, pour in the olive oil. Add the zucchini, mushrooms, onion, garlic powder, and Italian seasoning and sauté for 3 to 5 minutes, until the vegetables start to get some color.
3.   Season the vegetables with salt and pepper and add the beaten eggs. Cook for 1 minute on the stove and then transfer to the oven and cook for 8 to 10 minutes. The eggs should be nice and golden brown, but just cooked in the center.
4.   Top with the chopped tomato and transfer to 6 airtight containers and let cool. Store in the refrigerator for 4 to 5 days or freeze for 1 month.

SMART SHOPPING: I always buy my mushrooms in bulk instead of in the plastic containers. Then I only buy what I need, and nothing gets wasted.

Per serving: Calories: 197; Fat: 12g; Protein: 15g; Carbohydrates: 7g; Fiber: 2g

Oatmeal with Stewed Fruit

Makes 3 servings | Prep Time: 5 minutes | Cook Time: 20 minutes

There are many ways to prepare oatmeal, and it's one of the best breakfasts to keep the cost down. Plus, there's nothing better on a cold morning than a nice, hot bowl of oatmeal to get the day started. My version uses frozen fruit that is cooked with honey and ground cinnamon. This recipe also has sunflower seeds for added texture and protein. These ingredients are inexpensive, and all it takes to prepare this is some boiled water.

2 cups frozen berry medley (strawberries, raspberries, or blackberries)
2 teaspoons honey
½ teaspoon ground cinnamon

1½ cups quick oats
¼ cup raw or toasted sunflower seeds, shelled

1. In a small pot, combine the berries, honey, and cinnamon with ¼ cup of water. Let it come to a boil then reduce to a simmer and cook for 10 to 15 minutes. Transfer to 3 airtight containers and let cool.
2. Top each container of berries with ½ cup of oats and one-third of the sunflower seeds and store in the refrigerator for 4 to 5 days or freeze for 1 month.

SMART SHOPPING: You can buy quick oats and sunflower seeds in bulk.

Per serving: Calories: 281; Fat: 9g; Protein: 8g; Carbohydrates: 47g; Fiber: 8g

$2.75 PER PORTION

Deconstructed Beef and Mushroom Burger

· ·

Makes 3 servings | Prep Time: 15 minutes | Cook Time: 20 minutes

Burgers work well for inexpensive meal prepping. This version is a fun one—there is no bun, but there are roasted yam fries and lots of fresh toppings. The tomato and onion are served on the side, and the burger is topped with sautéed garlic and mushrooms.

⅔ **pound yams or sweet potatoes, cut into fries**
2 tablespoons olive oil, divided
2 teaspoons garlic powder, divided
1 teaspoon chili powder
1 teaspoon dried parsley
Salt

Freshly ground black pepper
⅔ **pound lean ground beef**
2 tablespoons unsalted butter
10 white button mushrooms, sliced
2 Roma tomatoes, sliced
¼ **cup sliced red onion**

1. Preheat the oven to 375°F. Line a baking sheet with parchment paper.
2. In a large bowl, toss the yams with 1 tablespoon of olive oil, 1 teaspoon of garlic powder, chili powder, and parsley, and season with salt and pepper. Arrange in a single layer on the prepared baking sheet. Bake for 20 minutes, mixing occasionally, until tender. Set aside.
3. Season the beef with salt and pepper. (You can test for flavor by cooking a tiny bit first over medium-high heat.) Form the meat into 3 patties.
4. In an oven-safe pan or skillet, heat the remaining 1 tablespoon of olive oil with the butter over medium-high heat. Sear the burgers until they are a golden-brown color on the outside, about 1 minute per side. Add the mushrooms and the remaining teaspoon of garlic powder to the pan, stir gently, and bake in the oven for 8 to 10 minutes. This will cook the burgers medium-well and the mushrooms will be nice and caramelized.
5. Portion the burgers and yams into 3 airtight containers. Top with the tomatoes and onion. Store in the refrigerator for 4 to 5 days or freeze for 1 month.

SWAP TO SAVE: Any ground meat works for this dish, and options like ground pork or chicken are even more cost-effective than beef.

Per serving: Calories: 409; Fat: 22g; Protein: 27g; Carbohydrates: 28g; Fiber: 5g

Vegetable Primavera Pasta, page 46

CHAPTER FOUR

Week 3

This week we add a variety of protein options. My intent is to show that you can cook within a budget and still be able to eat pricier proteins, such as turkey or seafood. Once again, we use a lot of frozen vegetables and two inexpensive breakfasts that keep this week under budget.

Week 3

	Breakfast	Lunch	Dinner
Monday	Fruit and Yogurt Parfait (page 48)	Clam and Potato Corn Chowder (page 47)	Chicken Fajita Rice Bowl (page 45)
Tuesday	Potato and Herb Pancakes (page 49)	Turkey Sliders with Sweet and Sour Peppers (page 50)	Vegetable Primavera Pasta (page 46)
Wednesday	Fruit and Yogurt Parfait	Clam and Potato Corn Chowder	Chicken Fajita Rice Bowl
Thursday	Potato and Herb Pancakes	Turkey Sliders with Sweet and Sour Peppers	Vegetable Primavera Pasta
Friday	Fruit and Yogurt Parfait	Clam and Potato Corn Chowder	Chicken Fajita Rice Bowl
Saturday	Potato and Herb Pancakes	Turkey Sliders with Sweet and Sour Peppers	Vegetable Primavera Pasta
Sunday	Fruit and Yogurt Parfait	Clam and Potato Corn Chowder	Chicken Fajita Rice Bowl

Shopping List

- Bell peppers, red (4)
- Garlic cloves (4)
- Mushrooms, white button (6)
- Onion, red, small (1)
- Onions, white, small (2)
- Potatoes, yellow (2 pounds)
- Scallions (1 small bunch)

DAIRY AND EGGS

- Butter, unsalted
  (2 tablespoons)
- Eggs, large (7)
- Greek yogurt, plain (2 cups)
- Milk, whole (4 ounces)
- Sour cream (½ cup)

MEAT AND SEAFOOD

- Chicken thighs (1 pound)
- Turkey, ground (12 ounces)

FROZEN

- Bell pepper and onion mix
  (8 ounces)
- Berry medley (12 ounces)
- Broccoli-cauliflower medley
  (8 ounces)
- Corn (8 ounces)
- Peas (4 ounces)

PANTRY

- Black pepper, ground
- Chicken stock (4 cups)
- Chili powder
- Cinnamon, ground
- Clams (2 [6.5-ounce] cans)
- Cumin, ground
- Dill, dried
- Garlic powder
- Golden raisins (4 ounces)
- Honey
- Italian seasoning
- Linguine (8 ounces)

- Olive oil
- Onion powder
- Salt
- Sunflower seeds (4 ounces)
- Vinegar, balsamic
- Vinegar, red wine
- White rice, medium-grain (4 ounces)

Prep It

1. Prepare the rice for the Chicken Fajita Rice Bowls (page 45) and cook the pasta for the Vegetable Primavera Pasta (page 46).

2. Prepare the vegetables for all recipes.

3. Prepare the Clam and Potato Corn Chowder (page 47) in its entirety.

4. Prepare the Fruit and Yogurt Parfaits (page 48) and make the Potato and Herb Pancakes (page 49).

5. Make the Turkey Sliders with Sweet and Sour Peppers (page 50) in its entirety.

6. Prepare the Vegetable Primavera Pasta, and the Chicken Fajita Rice Bowls.

ADDITIONAL OR MID-WEEK PREP

1. You can freeze the portions of the chowder and pull them out mid-week.

2. You can prep half the yogurt parfaits and half the potato pancakes on one day, and prep the other half later in the week.

3. Half of the pasta and rice can be packaged separately and frozen, then pulled out when the other portions of the primavera and fajita bowls will be served.

Chicken Fajita Rice Bowls

Makes 4 servings | Prep Time: 15 minutes | Cook Time: 30 minutes

There's nothing like the sound of the sizzling skillet filled with savory meat and vegetables. My fajitas taste like those you might find at a restaurant, except they are a bit more mindful of portion size and served over rice instead of in a tortilla. This bowl is full of peppers, onions, and juicy chicken thighs.

1½ cups water
¾ cup medium-grain white rice
Salt
2 tablespoons olive oil
1⅓ pounds boneless, skinless chicken
    thighs, cut into strips
2 red bell peppers, sliced

½ red onion, sliced
1 teaspoon garlic powder
1 teaspoon chili powder
1 teaspoon ground cumin
1 teaspoon onion powder
Freshly ground black pepper

1. In a small pot, combine the water and rice and salt lightly. Bring to a simmer over medium heat, then reduce the heat to low, cover, and cook for 25 minutes until the water has evaporated and the rice is nice and fluffy. Set aside to cool.
2. In a large pan over medium-high heat, pour in the olive oil. Add the chicken, bell peppers, and onion and sauté until the chicken is about 75 percent cooked and the vegetables have a lot of color in them, about 5 minutes.
3. Add the garlic powder, chili powder, cumin, onion powder, season with salt and pepper, and cook for another 2 to 3 minutes. Add a couple tablespoons of water and let everything simmer for another 1 to 2 minutes.
4. Add more salt and pepper, if needed, and portion into 4 airtight containers, along with the rice, and let cool. Store in the refrigerator for 4 to 5 days or freeze for 1 month.

SMART SHOPPING: Check for sales on other cuts of chicken that might be less expensive.

Per serving: Calories: 406; Fat: 14g; Protein: 33g; Carbohydrates: 36g; Fiber: 2g

Vegetable Primavera Pasta

Makes 3 servings | Prep Time: 10 minutes | Cook Time: 20 minutes

Primavera is a type of pasta that is enhanced by using a lot of seasonal vegetables and no thick tomato sauces. This dish utilizes several ingredients that work well for meal prepping on a budget, including frozen veggies, linguine noodles, and simple pantry ingredients. It comes together in just half an hour.

5 ounces linguine noodles

2 tablespoons olive oil, plus 1 teaspoon, divided

1 cup frozen bell pepper and onion mix, thawed

1 cup frozen broccoli and cauliflower florets, thawed

¼ cup frozen green peas, thawed

2 garlic cloves, sliced

2 tablespoons balsamic vinegar

1 teaspoon Italian seasoning

Salt

Freshly ground black pepper

1. Bring a large pot of salted water to boil. Cook the linguine, stirring often, for 8 to 10 minutes or according to package directions. The noodles should be firm to the bite but not fall apart. Drain, cool, and set aside.
2. In a large pan over medium-high heat, pour 2 tablespoons of olive oil and add the peppers and onions, broccoli and cauliflower, peas, and garlic. Cook for 2 to 3 minutes to caramelize the vegetables.
3. Add the balsamic vinegar to deglaze the pan and the Italian seasoning and reduce until the balsamic becomes a thick glaze, about 2 minutes.
4. Add the pasta and mix well. Add another teaspoon of olive oil to coat everything and season with salt and pepper. Cool and portion into 3 airtight containers. Store in the refrigerator for 4 to 5 days or freeze for 1 month.

PREP TIP: Making your own balsamic glaze as we did in step 3 is a neat, inexpensive hack so you don't have to buy it from a specialty store.

Per serving: Calories: 312; Fat: 11g; Protein: 9g; Carbohydrates: 44g; Fiber: 4g

Clam and Potato Corn Chowder

Makes 4 servings | Prep Time: 15 minutes | Cook Time: 30 minutes

Clam chowder is one of those simple dishes that smells delicious when simmered on the stove, filling your house with the tasty tang of seafood. Canned clams are conveniently inexpensive and loaded with protein, which makes this recipe a win for cheap and tasty meal prep. My version uses frozen corn, potatoes, and a touch of milk. The potatoes will thicken the soup as they cook so there is no need for any fancy thickeners.

2 tablespoons olive oil

½ cup diced white onion,
    ¼-inch pieces

1 teaspoon garlic powder

1 teaspoon dried dill

1 teaspoon chili powder

2 cups chicken stock

2 (6.5-ounce) cans clams

1½ cups diced yellow potato,
    ½-inch pieces

1 cup frozen corn

Salt

Freshly ground black pepper

½ cup whole milk

1. In a large stockpot over medium heat, pour in the olive oil. Add the onion and sauté for about 4 minutes, until they are almost transparent. Add the garlic powder, dill, and chili powder and cook for 1 minute.
2. Pour in the chicken stock, clams and their juices, potato, and corn and bring to a simmer. Cook for 25 to 30 minutes, mixing often to help the potatoes release their starch and thicken the soup.
3. Season with salt and pepper, then add the milk and let cool. Portion into 4 airtight containers and store in the refrigerator for 4 to 5 days or freeze for 1 month.

PREP TIP: When using canned clams, always keep the juices to add as extra flavoring.

Per serving: Calories: 274; Fat: 9g; Protein: 21g; Carbohydrates: 28g; Fiber: 3g

Fruit and Yogurt Parfait

- -

Makes 4 servings | Prep Time: 5 minutes, plus 10 minutes to thaw

Yogurt parfaits are a versatile breakfast option. All you need is good quality Greek yogurt and then you can add all sorts of toppings—such as seeds, fruit, and nuts—that allow for a lot of tastes and textures. My version uses some frozen fruit, raisins, and sunflower seeds, flavored with just a little bit of honey and ground cinnamon.

2 cups frozen berry medley (strawberries, raspberries, or blackberries)
2 cups reduced-fat plain Greek yogurt
¼ cup golden raisins

¼ cup raw or roasted sunflower seeds
1 teaspoon ground cinnamon
2 teaspoons honey

1. Let the berries thaw a bit first, about 10 minutes.
2. Divide the ingredients into each of 4 airtight containers. Start with the fruit on the bottom, then add a layer of yogurt, then raisins, then sunflower seeds, and top with ground cinnamon and honey. Store in the refrigerator for 4 days or freeze for 1 month.

SMART SHOPPING: Raisins can also be purchased in the bulk section, so you'll only need to buy what you need.

Per serving: Calories: 208; Fat: 7g; Protein: 9g; Carbohydrates: 30g; Fiber: 6g

Potato and Herb Pancakes

Makes 3 servings | Prep Time: 10 minutes | Cook Time: 10 minutes

These potato pancakes are something I've made for years, going all the way back to when I was a line cook at my first job. I like this version because grating everything makes it cook faster. I use grated potatoes, onions, and mushrooms to add a lot of flavor to the pancakes. Whisk in a couple eggs and you have a simple, inexpensive, balanced breakfast. They also look really fancy, so you'll impress your friends!

2 cups grated yellow potato

6 white button mushrooms, grated

6 large eggs, beaten

¼ white onion, grated

½ cup sliced scallions, both green and white parts

1 teaspoon garlic powder

1 teaspoon chili powder

Salt

Freshly ground black pepper

2 tablespoons olive oil

4 teaspoons sour cream, divided, for garnish

1. In a large bowl, combine the potato, mushrooms, eggs, onion, scallions, garlic powder, chili powder, salt, and pepper and mix well. Make sure to mix the "batter" after you make a pancake so there is an even amount of ingredients.
2. In a large pan, heat the olive oil over medium-high heat. You are aiming for 6 equal pancakes, about 4 inches in diameter.
3. Pour the batter into the pan, cooking 2 to 3 at a time, until golden brown on one side, about 3 minutes. Flip with a spatula and cook for another 3 minutes until brown on the other side.
4. Into each of 3 airtight containers, portion 2 pancakes with 1 teaspoon of sour cream off to the side. Store in the refrigerator for 4 to 5 days or freeze for 1 month.

SMART SHOPPING: You'll have sour cream left over from last week so it should work perfectly as a garnish for these pancakes. Also, don't buy your potatoes in bulk. Am I the only one who's bought a 5-pound bag that sat for weeks and turned mushy? Buying only as much as you need ensures that this doesn't happen.

Per serving: Calories: 335; Fat: 20g; Protein: 17g; Carbohydrates: 23g; Fiber: 4g

Turkey Sliders with Sweet and Sour Peppers

Makes 3 servings | Prep Time: 15 minutes | Cook Time: 15 minutes

Ground turkey is tasty, inexpensive, and works well with a lot of different flavors and ingredients. The richness of the turkey pairs well with the tangy sweetness of the sweet and sour peppers.

12 ounces ground turkey

1 large egg, beaten

Salt

Freshly ground black pepper

2 tablespoons olive oil, divided

2 tablespoons unsalted butter

2 garlic cloves, minced

2 red bell peppers, thinly sliced

½ red onion, thinly sliced

2 tablespoons red wine vinegar

1 tablespoon honey

1. In a medium bowl, mix the turkey and egg well. Season with salt and pepper and form into 6 small patties. Press them until they're nice and thin to speed up the cooking process.
2. In a large pan over medium-high heat, pour in 1 tablespoon of olive oil and cook the turkey sliders until they are golden brown, about 3 minutes per side.
3. Add the butter and garlic and let the butter melt. Once the butter and garlic brown a bit, take a spoon and baste the sliders with the butter to add moisture and flavor. Set aside and let cool.
4. Wipe down the pan and add the remaining 1 tablespoon of olive oil. Sauté the peppers and onion until they are nicely caramelized, about 5 minutes. Add the vinegar and honey and cook for 3 minutes. Let cool and divide the peppers between 3 airtight containers. Top each with 2 sliders and store in the refrigerator for 4 to 5 days or freeze for 1 month.

SMART SHOPPING: You can use fresh peppers and onion or frozen varieties to save time.

Per serving: Calories: 399; Fat: 28g; Protein: 25g; Carbohydrates: 13g; Fiber: 2g

Blackened Steak with Mushrooms and Rice, page 57

Blackened Steak with Mushrooms and Rice, page 57

CHAPTER FIVE

Week 4

Frozen vegetables makes this week extra budget-friendly. There are lots of tasty flavors—everything from a full-flavored vegetarian chili to an addictive blackened steak with mushrooms and rice.

Week 4

	Breakfast	Lunch	Dinner
Monday	Banana and Almond Breakfast Muffins (page 61)	Veggie Bean Chili (page 58)	Herbed Pork Chops with Brussels Sprouts and Zucchini (page 59)
Tuesday	Southwest Egg Bowl (page 62)	Ginger and Soy Salmon Rice Noodle Salad (page 60)	Blackened Steak with Mushrooms and Rice (page 57)
Wednesday	Banana and Almond Breakfast Muffins	Veggie Bean Chili	Herbed Pork Chops with Brussels Sprouts and Zucchini
Thursday	Southwest Egg Bowl	Ginger and Soy Salmon Rice Noodle Salad	Blackened Steak with Mushrooms and Rice
Friday	Banana and Almond Breakfast Muffins	Veggie Bean Chili	Herbed Pork Chops with Brussels Sprouts and Zucchini
Saturday	Southwest Egg Bowl	Ginger and Soy Salmon Rice Noodle Salad	Blackened Steak with Mushrooms and Rice
Sunday	Banana and Almond Breakfast Muffins	Veggie Bean Chili	Herbed Pork Chops with Brussels Sprouts and Zucchini

Shopping List

- Banana (1)
- Bell pepper, red (1)
- Brussels sprouts (1 pound)
- Dill (1 sprig)
- Garlic (2 cloves)
- Ginger (1-inch piece)
- Lime (1)
- Mushrooms, button (12)
- Onion, white (1 medium)
- Potato, yellow (1 large)
- Scallions (1 bunch)
- Thyme (2 sprigs)
- Tomatoes, Roma (3)
- Zucchini (1 pound)

DAIRY AND EGGS

- Butter (8 tablespoons)
- Eggs, large (8)

MEAT AND SEAFOOD

- Pork chops (1 pound)
- Sirloin tip steaks (12 ounces)

FROZEN

- Bell peppers (2 cups)
- Corn (1 cup)
- Edamame, shelled (½ cup)

PANTRY

- All-purpose flour (1 cup)
- Almonds, crushed (¼ cup)
- Baking powder
- Beans, kidney
  (1 [15-ounce] can)
- Black pepper, ground
- Brown sugar
- Chili powder
- Cumin, ground
- Garlic powder
- Honey
- Olive oil
- Rice noodles (⅔ cup)
- Salmon (1 [4-ounce] can)

- Salt
- Sesame oil
- Soy sauce

- Tomato sauce (3 cups)
- White rice, medium-grain (½ cup)

Prep It

1. Cook the rice for the Blackened Steak with Mushrooms and Rice (page 57), and also start the Veggie Bean Chili (page 58) cooking on the stove top.

2. Cut all the fresh vegetables for the Blackened Steak and the Herbed Pork Chops with Brussels Sprouts and Zucchini (page 59).

3. Cook the steaks and pork chops, and then cook the vegetables for their sides.

4. Cook the rice noodles (step 1) for the Ginger and Soy Salmon Rice Noodle Salad (page 60). Once cooked, assemble the salads.

5. Bake the Banana and Almond Breakfast Muffins (page 61) and make the Southwest Egg Bowls (page 62) in their entirety.

6. Let everything cool before packing into airtight containers.

ADDITIONAL OR MID-WEEK PREP

1. You can prepare the muffins ahead of time and freeze them. Just pull them out of the freezer to thaw in the refrigerator the day before you intend to eat them.

2. The salmon salad will last the week and can be prepared at the beginning of the week.

3. The chili will last a few months in the freezer, and meals can be pulled out the day before and put in the refrigerator to thaw before reheating.

Blackened Steak with Mushrooms and Rice

. . . .

Makes 3 servings | Prep Time: 10 minutes | Cook Time: 30 minutes

Steak can be tricky when it comes to eating on a budget. I always look for less popular but still tender cuts when shopping, such as flat iron, sirloin tip, and outside round. Portion size is often important, too, because thicker cuts increase the price (e.g., a 12-ounce New York strip steak). This dish is a simple blackened sirloin tip steak, served with garlicky mushrooms and light and fluffy rice.

1 cup water

½ cup medium-grain white rice

Salt

12 ounces sirloin tip steaks

1 teaspoon garlic powder, divided

Freshly ground black pepper

2 tablespoons olive oil

12 white button mushrooms, sliced

2 tablespoons unsalted butter

1 thyme sprig, leaves chopped

1. In a small pot, combine the water, rice, and a pinch of salt. Bring it to a boil, then cover and reduce the heat to a simmer. Cook for 20 to 25 minutes, or until the rice is just light and fluffy and the water has all evaporated.
2. Season the steaks with ½ teaspoon of garlic powder and salt and pepper.
3. In a large pan over medium-high heat, pour the olive oil and heat until almost smoking, then add the steaks. Cook for 3 to 4 minutes per side for medium-rare, or to desired doneness.
4. Transfer the steaks to a plate and let rest. To the same pan, add the mushrooms, butter, the remaining ½ teaspoon of garlic powder, and thyme and cook for 5 to 6 minutes, until the mushrooms are well caramelized. Add more salt and pepper to taste, if desired.
5. Portion into 3 airtight containers. Store for up to 4 to 5 days in the refrigerator and up to 1 month in the freezer.

SMART SHOPPING: There are often sales on red meat. Keep an eye out for the best price on different steak cuts.

Per serving: Calories: 440; Fat: 24g; Protein: 29g; Carbohydrates: 29g; Fiber: 1g

Veggie Bean Chili

. . . .

Makes 4 servings | Prep Time: 10 minutes | Cook Time: 25 minutes

Chili is a hearty and inexpensive way to get healthy proteins and vegetables into your diet. It's also an easy dish to create and can just simmer on your stove without needing much attention. I've made versions of this chili with ground turkey, pork, and even with juicy chunks of steak. This version is vegetarian and uses lots of beans, frozen veggies, and a tasty tomato sauce. I also add some freshly chopped tomatoes right at the end, as well.

2 tablespoons olive oil
1 cup frozen bell peppers, thawed
½ cup frozen corn, thawed
½ cup diced white onion
1 teaspoon chili powder
1 teaspoon garlic powder
1 teaspoon ground cumin

3 cups tomato sauce
1 (15-ounce) can red kidney
    beans, drained
½ cup water
½ cup chopped Roma tomatoes
Salt
Freshly ground black pepper

1. In a large pot over medium-high heat, pour in the olive oil. When hot, combine the peppers, corn, onion, chili powder, garlic powder, and cumin and cook for 3 to 4 minutes, until softened and lightly colored.
2. Pour in the tomato sauce, beans, and water. Mix well and let it come to a gentle simmer. Cook for 20 minutes. (You may want to put a lid on the pot to prevent bubbling or splatters.)
3. Add the fresh tomatoes and cook for another 5 minutes. Season with salt and pepper.
4. Portion into 4 airtight containers and let cool in the refrigerator. This will keep for 5 days in the refrigerator or up to 2 months in the freezer.

SWAP TO SAVE: You can use any type of canned bean for this. You can also substitute for the same volume of dry beans, which are cheaper. You'll have the added step of soaking them overnight.

Per serving: Calories: 234; Fat: 8g; Protein: 10g; Carbohydrates: 35g; Fiber: 10g

Herbed Pork Chops with Brussels Sprouts and Zucchini

$2.75 PER PORTION

Makes 4 servings | Prep Time: 10 minutes | Cook Time: 25 minutes

Pork is an inexpensive meat that's full of flavor. Growing up, I ate barbecued pork chops often, but the problem was that my parents loved the pork well done! With this recipe, I guarantee that the pork chops will be nice and moist. Plus, it uses only one pan, so cleanup is a breeze.

2 tablespoons olive oil
1 pound pork chops
Salt
Freshly ground black pepper
½ teaspoon garlic powder
1 pound Brussels sprouts, stemmed and quartered

1 pound zucchini, cut into ½-inch chunks
1 thyme sprig, chopped
1 dill sprig, chopped
2 teaspoons unsalted butter

1. Preheat the oven to 375°F.
2. In a large, oven-safe pan over medium-high heat, pour in the olive oil. Season the pork chops with salt, pepper, and garlic powder, and add to the pan carefully once the oil is almost smoking.
3. Cook the pork for 2 minutes per side, assuming about ½-inch thickness. Add the Brussels sprouts and zucchini and sprinkle the fresh thyme and dill on top, covering the pork and the vegetables. Season the veggies with salt and pepper, if desired.
4. Bake for 10 minutes. Take the pan out, add the butter, and cook for another 10 minutes, until the vegetables are brightly colored and the pork registers 145°F.
5. Let cool and transfer to 4 airtight containers. Store for 4 to 5 days in the refrigerator or freeze for up to 1 month.

SWAP TO SAVE: Grocery stores usually offer sales for certain cuts of pork, aside from chops. Keep a look out for the best price because this recipe works with all cuts.

Per serving: Calories: 290; Fat: 13g; Protein: 31g; Carbohydrates: 14g; Fiber: 6g

Ginger and Soy Salmon Rice Noodle Salad

Makes 3 servings | Prep Time: 10 minutes | Cook Time: 25 minutes

This is one of my favorite recipes in the whole book. Canned salmon is a healthy, inexpensive option that can be enhanced with other flavors. Only one can of salmon is needed for these 3 portions since you'll also get protein from the edamame beans. This feels like a fancy salad, but it's very price-conscious!

⅔ cup dry rice noodles
1 teaspoon olive oil (optional)
1 (4-ounce) can boneless, skinless
   salmon, drained
½ cup frozen shelled edamame, thawed
½ cup sliced scallions, both green and
   white parts

½ red bell pepper, thinly sliced
1 tablespoon soy sauce
2 garlic cloves, minced
1 teaspoon grated ginger
1 teaspoon honey
½ teaspoon sesame oil
1 tablespoon freshly squeezed lime juice

1. Bring a medium pot of water to boil and cook the rice noodles for 4 to 5 minutes, stirring often because they stick easily. Drain and cool. (Add 1 teaspoon of olive oil to the pot to help with sticking, if desired.)
2. In a large bowl, combine the noodles, salmon, edamame, scallions, and bell pepper and mix well.
3. In a separate bowl, whisk the soy sauce, garlic, ginger, honey, and sesame oil together to make the dressing. Add it to the noodles and salmon bowl and mix well.
4. Add the lime juice and stir once more. Transfer to 3 airtight containers and store in the refrigerator for up to 4 days. This salad is not recommended for freezing.

SMART SHOPPING: Frozen edamame beans are a great, inexpensive source of protein.

Per serving: Calories: 241; Fat: 4g; Protein: 13g; Carbohydrates: 39g; Fiber: 3g

Banana and Almond Breakfast Muffins

Makes 8 muffins | Prep Time: 10 minutes | Cook Time: 15 minutes

I love making muffins for breakfasts. They're easy to batch-cook for the entire week and then grab when you are heading out the door. Muffins can be a healthy option, too, when eaten in proper portions and made from scratch, as these are. This recipe uses crushed almonds and a ripe banana. The key to keeping the cost down is purchasing a small quantity of almonds in bulk and crushing them so they can be evenly distributed.

Olive oil, for greasing
1 cup all-purpose flour, sifted
¼ cup brown sugar
1 teaspoon baking powder
1 banana, mashed

2 large eggs, well beaten
¼ cup butter, melted
¼ cup crushed almonds
¼ cup water
Salt

1. Preheat the oven to 375°F. Grease 8 cups of a muffin tin with olive oil and set aside.
2. In a large bowl, sift the flour, brown sugar, and baking powder.
3. Add the banana, eggs, butter, almonds, and water and season with a bit of salt.
4. Pour the mixture into the greased muffin cups and bake for 15 to 18 minutes, or until a toothpick inserted in the center comes out clean.
5. Let cool and place 2 muffins each into 4 airtight containers. Store up to 5 days in the refrigerator or up to 1 month in the freezer.

SWAP TO SAVE: You can replace almonds with another nut, such as cashews or walnuts.

Per serving (2 muffins): Calories: 347; Fat: 17g; Protein: 8g; Carbohydrates: 42g; Fiber: 2g

Southwest Egg Bowl

Makes 3 servings | Prep Time: 5 minutes | Cook Time: 10 minutes

Egg bowls are a great way to eat lots of healthy vegetables, as well as inexpensive protein. It's a simple breakfast that is prepared in 15 minutes. My version of an egg bowl has a Southwest theme, with peppers, corn, and tasty spices to add a bit of heat. The key to this dish is the crispy, hash brown–style potatoes served with light and fluffy scrambled eggs.

2 tablespoons olive oil
1 cup frozen bell peppers, thawed
¼ cup frozen corn
¼ cup grated white onion
½ teaspoon chili powder
½ teaspoon garlic powder
Salt

Freshly ground black pepper
1 large yellow potato, grated
6 large eggs, well beaten
¼ cup sliced scallions, both green and white parts
1 Roma tomato, diced, for garnish

1. In a large pan over medium-high heat, pour in the olive oil. Add the peppers and corn and cook for 1 minute to get some of the moisture out. Add the onion, chili powder, garlic powder, salt, and pepper and cook for 1 to 2 minutes.
2. With a paper towel, squeeze out some of the moisture from the potatoes and add them to the pan. Season with salt and pepper.
3. Mix well and cook until the potatoes are brown on one side, about 3 minutes. Once brown, flip and cook for another 3 minutes.
4. Add the eggs and scramble together until they solidify and become nice and fluffy. Store in 3 airtight containers in the refrigerator for 4 days, and garnish with the scallions and tomato.

SWAP TO SAVE: Instead of fresh grated potato, you could also use frozen shredded hash browns. There is less labor involved, and it's easier to squeeze out the moisture when the potatoes are thawed.

Per serving: Calories: 356; Fat: 19g; Protein: 17g; Carbohydrates: 31g; Fiber: 5g

One-Pan Shrimp and Veggies, page 94

Part Two

Bonus Meal Prep Recipes

Now that you've gone through four weeks of meal preps, I wanted to make sure you have plenty of other great recipes to continue your price-conscious meal prep journey! Add any of these recipes to your weekly roster, or swap in with any of the previous weekly preps where you see fit.

Breakfast

CHAPTER SIX

Breakfast

Berry Medley and Banana Smoothie

Makes 4 servings | Prep Time: 5 minutes

Smoothies are a simple, fast way to make breakfast in the morning, especially if you have a busy day ahead. Just add some healthy ingredients in a blender and in seconds you have a good start to the day! Smoothies are perfect for meal prepping on a budget, and the oats and almond milk make it creamy and filling.

2 cups frozen berry medley (any kind)
1 cup quick oats
2 bananas, sliced

2 teaspoons honey
4 scoops protein powder (optional)
4 cups plain unsweetened almond milk

1. Divide and place the berries, oats, bananas, honey, and protein powder (if using) into 4 airtight containers and place in the freezer.
2. On the morning you'll be serving the smoothie, take out a frozen portion and add it and 1 cup of almond milk to a blender. Blend until smooth. If it's too thick, you may have to add some water.

SWAP TO SAVE: Plain almond milk is inexpensive and doesn't change the flavor of the smoothie too much, but you could also opt for dairy milk or water.

Per serving: Calories: 244; Fat: 4g; Protein: 10g; Carbohydrates: 46g; Fiber: 9g

Banana-Orange Breakfast Smoothie

Makes 4 servings | Prep Time: 5 minutes

This is another fast smoothie recipe that uses simple ingredients. Unlike the Berry Medley and Banana Smoothie (page 68), the fruit starts out at room temperature and is frozen with the other ingredients to make storing simple and easy.

4 cups plain unsweetened almond milk

4 small oranges, peeled, diced, and frozen

2 bananas, sliced

1 cup quick oats

4 scoops protein powder (optional)

2 teaspoons honey

1. Divide and place the almond milk, oranges, banana slices, oats, protein powder (if using), and honey into 4 resealable containers or jars and freeze.
2. Transfer 1 portion to the refrigerator the night before you're going to drink it. In the morning, pour it into a blender. Blend until smooth. If it's too thick, you may have to add some water.
3. Store unblended portions in the freezer for up to 1 month. Once blended, they shouldn't stay in the refrigerator longer than 1 day.

SMART SHOPPING: Oranges are a great fruit you wouldn't usually think of adding to a smoothie, but they add a nice citrus flavor.

Per serving: Calories: 276; Fat: 4g; Protein: 11g; Carbohydrates: 56g; Fiber: 8g

Granola Fruit Cups

Makes 3 servings | Prep Time: 5 minutes | Cook Time: 15 minutes

Granola is a versatile breakfast option because you can add many different flavors and textures to it, such as fresh, dried, or frozen fruit, yogurt, nuts, seeds, and even cottage cheese! It's convenient, too, and easy to find ingredients in the bulk section at grocery stores to whip up a different version each time. This version comes together in under 20 minutes and uses dried fruit, seeds, and frozen fruit.

Olive oil, for greasing
1 tablespoon butter
1 cup quick oats
¼ cup raw sunflower seeds
¼ cup raisins

2 teaspoons honey
½ teaspoon ground cinnamon
2 cups frozen berries (any kind), thawed
2 cups frozen chopped apples, thawed
Salt

1. Preheat the oven to 350°F. Grease a baking sheet with olive oil or line it with parchment paper.
2. In a medium heat-safe bowl, melt the butter in the microwave for about 20 seconds, then mix with the oats, sunflower seeds, raisins, honey, and cinnamon until well combined.
3. Transfer to the prepared baking sheet and bake for 10 minutes until lightly roasted. Let cool.
4. Portion out the granola into 4 airtight containers. Top with the thawed fruit.
5. Store in the refrigerator for up to 4 days. If freezing, don't thaw the frozen fruit before topping the granola. The granola will keep in the freezer for up to 1 month.

SMART SHOPPING: All the dry ingredients can be found in bulk at most grocery stores. This will ensure that you only have to buy what you need.

Per serving: Calories: 379; Fat: 15g; Protein: 8g; Carbohydrates: 61g; Fiber: 12g

Cottage Cheese and Applesauce Parfait

Makes 4 servings | Prep Time: 5 minutes | Cook Time: 10 minutes

Cottage cheese was something I never ate as a kid. But after I rediscovered it as an adult, I realized that cottage cheese is a great, inexpensive, and filling protein option for breakfast. Sometimes it's just a little too plain. To fancy it up, this recipe uses a homemade applesauce that pairs perfectly with the saltiness of the cottage cheese. This is a complete breakfast, and the combination can be pretty addictive!

4 cups frozen chopped apples
½ cup water
2 tablespoons honey

1 tablespoon butter
½ teaspoon ground cinnamon
2 cups whole milk cottage cheese

1. In a large pot over medium heat, combine the apples, water, honey, butter, and cinnamon. Bring to a simmer and cook until the apples are soft enough to mash, about 10 minutes.
2. Use a potato masher or fork to mash the apples until smooth. Let cool.
3. Portion the cottage cheese into 4 airtight containers and top with the applesauce. This parfait will last up to 1 week in the refrigerator, and is not recommended for freezing.

SWAP TO SAVE: You could also use fresh apples because it may be more practical than buying a whole bag of frozen apples.

Per serving: Calories: 371; Fat: 20g; Protein: 15g; Carbohydrates: 37g; Fiber: 3g

$1.50 PER PORTION

Orange-Cranberry Muffins

Makes 6 muffins | Prep Time: 5 minutes | Cook Time: 20 minutes

Muffins are a great option for a quick grab-and-go breakfast. These orange-cranberry muffins are easy to prep and can be made in larger batches and frozen, so you always have breakfast ready to go any day of the week. This simple recipe uses freshly squeezed orange juice and dried cranberries.

Olive oil, for greasing
1 cup all-purpose flour, sifted
¼ cup brown sugar
1 teaspoon baking powder
½ teaspoon ground cinnamon
½ cup dried cranberries

2 large eggs, well beaten
¼ cup butter, melted
¼ cup freshly squeezed orange juice
　(from about 1 orange)
Zest of 1 orange

1. Preheat the oven to 375°F. Grease a 6-cup muffin tin with olive oil and set aside.
2. In a large bowl, sift together the flour, brown sugar, baking powder, and cinnamon.
3. Add the cranberries, eggs, butter, orange juice, and zest, and mix gently. (Don't overmix because it can make the muffins tough.)
4. Divide the batter between the muffin tins and bake for 18 to 20 minutes, until a toothpick inserted in the center comes out clean.
5. Portion into 3 airtight containers or resealable bags. These muffins will last up to 5 days in the refrigerator or up to 1 month in the freezer.

SWAP TO SAVE: You can use golden sugar if you don't have brown sugar for this recipe.

Per serving: Calories: 226; Fat: 10g; Protein: 4g; Carbohydrates: 31g; Fiber: 1g

Homemade Fruity White Chocolate Granola Bars

$1.25 PER PORTION

Makes 6 bars | Prep Time: 10 minutes | Cook Time: 10 minutes

A granola bar is an easy breakfast that is perfect for grabbing and going. You need basic ingredients, like oats and honey, and then can add nuts, seeds, and fruit to make them any way you like. Granola bars are also great because you can make large batches and store them in the freezer. Pull out a granola bar each morning and boom! Breakfast is served.

¼ cup honey
2 tablespoons brown sugar
1 tablespoon unsalted butter
2 cups quick oats

½ cup dried cranberries
½ cup raisins
⅓ cup white chocolate chips
Salt

1. In a large pot over medium heat, combine the honey, brown sugar, and butter. Cook until everything melts and starts to bubble, about 4 minutes.
2. Remove the pot from the heat and add the oats, cranberries, raisins, and white chocolate chips and stir to combine.
3. Season with a touch of salt and transfer to a 8-inch square casserole dish.
4. Let cool for 2 to 3 hours. Cut into 6 even pieces and store in airtight containers in the refrigerator for up to 1 week or in the freezer for 1 month.

SWAP TO SAVE: You can use any dried fruit for this recipe, such as apricots, peaches, or even chopped dates.

Per serving (1 bar): Calories: 272; Fat: 7g; Protein: 5g; Carbohydrates: 52g; Fiber: 3g

Egg and Bean Breakfast Wraps

Makes 4 servings | Prep Time: 5 minutes | Cook Time: 5 minutes

I am obsessed with breakfast wraps. When I was working in kitchens, it was one of the fastest ways to eat breakfast or lunch and then get back to a busy workday. For these, all you need are one or two eggs, some fresh or frozen ingredients, and a small tortilla, and breakfast is served! To keep things a bit healthier for this one, I use one egg per portion, but black beans add additional protein, and veggies up the nutritional content.

1 tablespoon unsalted butter
1 teaspoon olive oil
¼ cup diced red onion
¼ cup frozen corn
¼ cup frozen bell peppers

4 large eggs, well beaten
½ cup canned black beans
Salt
Freshly ground black pepper
4 (8-inch) flour tortillas

1. In a large nonstick pan, heat the butter and olive oil over medium-high heat. Add the onion, corn, and peppers and sauté for 3 to 4 minutes. The veggies should be nicely caramelized.
2. Add the eggs and beans and scramble until the eggs solidify and are light and fluffy. Season with salt and pepper.
3. Distribute the egg mixture between the tortillas, fold in the sides, and roll them up. Store in airtight containers in the refrigerator for 3 to 4 days or wrapped in plastic wrap, then aluminum foil in the freezer for 1 month. The double wrapping helps prevent freezer burn.

SWAP TO SAVE: There are many types of tortillas. Look for the best priced 8-inch size.

Per serving: Calories: 310; Fat: 12g; Protein: 13g; Carbohydrates: 36g; Fiber: 4g

Hash Brown Egg Cups

Makes 8 cups | Prep Time: 10 minutes | Cook Time: 12 minutes

My first kitchen job was as a breakfast cook, and I loved cooking eggs and making crispy hash browns best. This recipe combines the two into an inexpensive breakfast option that is tasty and filling. It's also convenient because these egg cups are essentially savory muffins full of flavor.

2 tablespoons olive oil, plus more for greasing
1 large yellow potato, grated
4 white button mushrooms, grated
1 teaspoon garlic powder

Salt
Freshly ground black pepper
¼ cup sliced scallions, both green and white parts
8 large eggs, well beaten

1. Preheat the oven to 400°F. Grease 8 cups of a muffin tin with olive oil and set aside.
2. In a large pan over medium-high heat, pour in the olive oil, then add the potatoes and mushrooms.
3. Season with the garlic powder, salt, and pepper and sauté the vegetables until golden brown and well caramelized, about 4 minutes.
4. Divide the veggie mixture evenly between the greased muffin cups. Sprinkle with the scallions and divide the eggs among the cups.
5. Bake for 10 to 12 minutes until the outside is golden brown and the inside is just cooked.
6. Let cool and transfer to 4 airtight containers. Once cooled, store for up to 4 days in the refrigerator or up to 1 month in the freezer.

SMART SHOPPING: Alternatively, instead of buying a carton of eggs, you can buy liquid egg that is already premixed.

Per serving (2 egg cups): Calories: 282; Fat: 16g; Protein: 15g; Carbohydrates: 18g; Fiber: 2g

Mushroom, Tomato, and Basil Omelet

Makes 4 servings | Prep Time: 5 minutes | Cook Time: 5 minutes

Eggs are versatile, cheap, and great for meal prep. One of my favorite combinations for omelets is this Italian-inspired dish. Fresh herbs, tomatoes, and mushrooms make this a satisfying omelet.

1 tablespoon olive oil
1 cup chopped Roma tomatoes
12 white button mushrooms, sliced
1 cup sliced red onion

Salt
Freshly ground black pepper
6 fresh basil leaves, torn
12 large eggs, well beaten

1. In a large pan over medium-high heat, pour in the olive oil, then add the tomatoes, mushrooms, and onion. Cook for 2 to 3 minutes until the mushrooms and onion start to caramelize and the tomatoes start to break down.
2. Season with salt and pepper, then add the torn basil leaves and let cook for 30 seconds.
3. Add the eggs and swirl around in the pan. Use a spatula to scrape the egg from around the pan to make sure that all the liquid is cooked.
4. Flip the omelet and cook for another 30 seconds. The egg should be slightly browned for added flavor.
5. Transfer to 4 airtight containers and let cool. Store the omelet for 3 to 4 days in the refrigerator. I don't recommend freezing.

SMART SHOPPING: Many grocery stores sell small basil plants that will yield basil for weeks or months. This is often cheaper in the long run than buying small bunches of fresh basil.

Per serving: Calories: 276; Fat: 18g; Protein: 21g; Carbohydrates: 7g; Fiber: 2g

CHAPTER SEVEN

Lunch and Dinner

Chili-Lemon Tuna Cakes, Red Lentils, and Sautéed Zucchini

Makes 4 servings | Prep Time: 15 minutes | Cook Time: 30 minutes

There are many other ways to use a can of tuna besides tuna salad. I keep two to three cans in my pantry for recipes like this one that is easy. The balance of the red lentils and smaller tuna cakes provides filling protein but keeps the costs down per portion. The cakes are sweet and flavorful, and the zucchini is cooked simply with olive oil, salt, and pepper.

2 (5-ounce) cans flaked white
    tuna, drained
2 large eggs
¼ cup diced red onion
2 teaspoons freshly squeezed
    lemon juice
1 teaspoon dried dill
1 teaspoon honey

½ teaspoon red pepper flakes
Salt
Freshly ground black pepper
3 tablespoons olive oil, divided
¾ cup dry red lentils
2 medium zucchini, chopped into
    ½-inch chunks

1. Preheat the oven to 375°F.
2. In a small bowl, mix the tuna, eggs, onion, lemon juice, dill, honey, and red pepper flakes. Season with salt and pepper and portion into 4 equal tuna cakes.
3. In a large, oven-safe pan over medium-high heat, pour in 2 tablespoons of olive oil. Sear the tuna cakes on each side for about 2 minutes each, until they are nicely browned. Then transfer the pan to the oven for 8 minutes. Let cool and set aside on a plate.
4. In a medium pot, combine 1½ cups of cold water and the lentils. Season with salt and let it come to a simmer. Cook for 15 minutes or until the lentils are tender.

5. Using the same pan as the tuna cakes over medium-high heat, pour in the remaining tablespoon of olive oil and the zucchini. Season with salt and pepper and sauté for 3 to 4 minutes until golden brown.

6. Portion the tuna cakes, lentils, and zucchini into 4 airtight containers. Store in the refrigerator for 4 to 5 days.

SMART SHOPPING: Lentils are often cheaper when purchased in bulk.

Per serving: Calories: 355; Fat: 15g; Protein: 26g; Carbohydrates: 29g; Fiber: 5g

Spicy White Bean Minestrone Soup

Makes 4 servings | Prep Time: 15 minutes | Cook Time: 30 minutes

Soup can be a great option when cooking on a budget. You can add all kinds of inexpensive ingredients, such as frozen vegetables, tougher cuts of meat, and even make your own stock using leftover vegetables. This soup is a take on a classic minestrone, using tasty white kidney beans and lots of vegetables. It's a hearty soup that doesn't break the bank.

2 tablespoons olive oil
1 medium zucchini, chopped
½ cup chopped white onion
4 garlic cloves, minced
2 cups frozen vegetable medley
½ cup chopped Roma tomatoes
1 tablespoon balsamic vinegar

4 cups vegetable stock
1 (15-ounce) can white kidney beans, drained
2 teaspoons Italian seasoning
Salt
Freshly ground black pepper

1. In a large pot over medium-high heat, pour in the olive oil, then add the zucchini, onion, and garlic. Sauté for 3 to 4 minutes, until softened.
2. Add the frozen vegetables and tomatoes and cook for another 2 minutes, until the vegetables are caramelized.
3. Pour in the balsamic vinegar and deglaze the pan by scraping up the brown bits with a wooden spoon. Add the vegetable stock, beans, and Italian seasoning.
4. Simmer for 15 to 20 minutes until the flavors are infused. Season with salt and pepper and serve.

SMART SHOPPING: Bags of frozen vegetables are perfect for sides or additions to soup. They last longer than fresh vegetables and retain more of their nutrients when frozen.

Per serving: Calories: 231; Fat: 7g; Protein: 10g; Carbohydrates: 33g; Fiber: 9g

Ground Turkey Chili

Makes 4 servings | Prep Time: 15 minutes | Cook Time: 30 minutes

Chili is such a simple dish to create with minimal ingredients. It's also easy to vary the kinds of beans, veggies, and proteins you use. My version uses ground turkey and red kidney beans. I also added veggies, frozen and fresh, to make this a really hearty dish. You will keep the cost down by adding less meat.

$2.50 PER PORTION

2 tablespoons olive oil
12 ounces ground turkey
½ cup chopped white onion
½ cup frozen corn
½ cup frozen bell peppers
3 garlic cloves, finely chopped

1 teaspoon chili powder
½ teaspoon ground cumin
3 cups tomato sauce
¾ cup canned red kidney beans, drained
Salt
Freshly ground black pepper

1. In a large pot over medium-high heat, pour in the olive oil. Add the turkey, breaking up the meat, and cook for 4 to 5 minutes until mostly browned.
2. Add the onion, corn, peppers, garlic, chili powder, and cumin and cook for 3 to 5 minutes to caramelize the vegetables and bring out the flavor of the garlic and spices. Mix well and make sure not to burn the garlic.
3. Add the tomato sauce and beans and mix well. Add ¼ cup of water and bring to a simmer. Cook for 25 to 30 minutes to really develop the flavors. Add salt and pepper to taste.
4. Portion evenly into 4 airtight containers and let cool. This will cool the chili quicker than cooling down the whole pot. Store the chili for 4 to 5 days in the refrigerator or up to 2 months in the freezer.

SWAP TO SAVE: You can use ground chicken or turkey in this version, whichever is cheaper.

Per serving: Calories: 311; Fat: 15g; Protein: 22g; Carbohydrates: 26g; Fiber: 7g

Budget Beef Stroganoff

Makes 4 servings | Prep Time: 10 minutes | Cook Time: 20 minutes

I remember the first time I made stroganoff in culinary school and absolutely fell in love! Granted we were using demi-glace, full-fat sour cream, and tender sliced beef, but I always remember the sweet, salty, and sour taste of this dish. I've made it various ways over the years, but this version is inexpensive without sacrificing taste.

1 tablespoon olive oil
12 ounces lean ground beef
8 white button mushrooms, sliced
2 tablespoons diced white onion
1 teaspoon garlic powder
½ cup beef stock

2 dill pickles, diced
3 tablespoons sour cream
7 ounces dry egg noodles
Salt
Freshly ground black pepper

1. In a large pan over medium-high heat, pour in the olive oil. Add the beef and cook for about 7 minutes, until well browned.
2. Add the mushrooms, onion, and garlic powder and sauté for 3 to 5 minutes, until the vegetables are well caramelized and you can smell the garlic.
3. Pour in the beef stock and let it reduce by half to develop the flavor and cook the beef further.
4. Add the pickles and sour cream, then reduce the heat to low and let the sauce thicken for 2 to 3 minutes. Season to taste with salt and pepper.
5. Bring a medium pot of salted water to a boil and cook the egg noodles according to package directions. Drain and toss into the pan with the beef and veggies. Mix well, coating the noodles with the sauce.
6. Portion equally into 4 airtight containers and let cool completely. Store for 3 to 4 days in the refrigerator or up to 1 month in the freezer.

SWAP TO SAVE: Egg noodles are usually inexpensive, but you can substitute with any pasta you prefer.

Per serving: Calories: 370; Fat: 12g; Protein: 27g; Carbohydrates: 39g; Fiber: 3g

Simple Chicken Stir-Fry with a Ginger-Soy Sauce

. . . .

Makes 4 servings | Prep Time: 15 minutes | Cook Time: 30 minutes

When it comes to eating on a budget, nothing beats a good stir-fry. You can add all kinds of vegetables, any simple protein, and your favorite sauces, rice, or noodles, and you're good to go! Stir-fries are filling and use a lot of inexpensive ingredients, like frozen veggies and cheaper proteins. This version uses chicken thighs, frozen broccoli and bell peppers, and a quick and easy stir-fry sauce.

2 cups water
1⅓ cups medium-grain white rice
1 tablespoon olive oil
12 ounces boneless skinless chicken thighs, sliced
8 white button mushrooms, sliced

1 cup frozen bell peppers
1 cup frozen broccoli florets
3 garlic cloves, finely chopped
1 teaspoon grated fresh ginger
2 tablespoons soy sauce
1 tablespoon honey

1. In a small pot, combine the water and rice over medium heat. Bring to a simmer, then reduce the heat to low, cover, and cook for 25 to 30 minutes, until the water has evaporated and the rice is nice and fluffy. Let cool.
2. In a large nonstick pan over high heat, pour in the olive oil. Add the chicken thighs and cook.
3. After 2 to 3 minutes, add the mushrooms, bell peppers, broccoli, garlic, and ginger and cook for another 3 to 4 minutes. The mushrooms should have some color on them.
4. Add the soy sauce and honey and let simmer for 1 minute. Transfer to 4 airtight containers, along with the cooked rice. Store for 4 to 5 days in the refrigerator or 1 month in the freezer.

SWAP TO SAVE: You can use fresh or frozen produce for this recipe.

Per serving: Calories: 413; Fat: 8g; Protein: 24g; Carbohydrates: 61g; Fiber: 3g

Tuna Salad Wraps

. . . .

Makes 4 servings | Prep Time: 10 minutes

Tuna salad is such a simple, filling, and inexpensive meal. It works for lunch and dinner and it's easy to make it your own. My version uses crunchy celery and red onion, with a tasty dill mayo and fresh lemon juice.

2 (5-ounce) cans flaked white tuna,
    drained
2 tablespoons mayonnaise
¼ cup diced celery
¼ cup diced red onion
1 tablespoon chopped fresh or dried dill
1 tablespoon freshly squeezed
    lemon juice

½ teaspoon garlic powder
Salt
Freshly ground black pepper
4 (10-inch) flour tortillas
1 cup thinly sliced cucumber, divided

1. In a large bowl, combine the tuna, mayo, celery, onion, dill, lemon juice, garlic powder, salt, and pepper.
2. On each tortilla, place ¼ cup of cucumber slices. Top with the tuna mixture, fold the sides in, and roll up.
3. The wraps will stay fresh for 3 to 4 days in the refrigerator. You can also store the tuna mixture in the refrigerator separately and assemble the tortillas the day you plan on eating them.

SWAP TO SAVE: Fresh or dried dill works for this recipe. Use whatever you have on hand.

Per serving: Calories: 364; Fat: 12g; Protein: 20g; Carbohydrates: 42g; Fiber: 3g

Creamy Chicken Broccoli Soup

Makes 4 servings | Prep Time: 10 minutes | Cook Time: 30 minutes

There's nothing I love more on a cold day than a hot cup of soup. A creamy broccoli soup happens to be one of my favorites. This soup is perfect for inexpensive meal prep because frozen broccoli works well here. To make things heartier, I add some chicken thighs, so it really becomes a full meal in a bowl. It's easy to make and even easier to eat!

$2.25 PER PORTION

1 tablespoon olive oil
12 ounces boneless, skinless chicken thighs, cut into 1-inch pieces
¼ cup finely chopped white onion
½ teaspoon garlic powder
2 cups chicken stock, divided
1 cup heavy whipping cream

2 cups frozen broccoli florets
2 tablespoons cornstarch
1 tablespoon freshly squeezed lemon juice
Salt
Freshly ground black pepper

1. In a large pot over medium heat, pour the olive oil. Add the chicken thighs, but don't let them brown since this will be a light-colored soup.
2. Add the onion and garlic powder and let cook for another 2 to 3 minutes, until the onion is translucent.
3. Pour 1¾ cups of the stock and the heavy cream into the pot and bring to a simmer. Simmer for 5 to 10 minutes, add the broccoli, and simmer for 2 more minutes, until the broccoli turns bright green.
4. In a small bowl, whisk the cornstarch and the remaining ¼ cup of stock to make a slurry. Add it to the soup and let it simmer and thicken until it coats the back of a spoon.
5. Season with lemon juice, salt, and pepper. Let cool and portion into 4 airtight containers. Store the soup for 4 to 5 days in the refrigerator or up to 1 month in the freezer.

SMART SHOPPING: If I'm making a really large batch of this soup, I buy pre-cooked whole chicken and shred the meat.

Per serving: Calories: 380; Fat: 29g; Protein: 20g; Carbohydrates: 10g; Fiber: 3g

Blackened Chicken with Roasted Zucchini and Brussels Sprouts

Makes 4 servings | Prep Time: 10 minutes | Cook Time: 30 minutes

All the ingredients in this blackened chicken recipe are cooked in one pan. Lots of tasty spices flavor the chicken, and the Brussels sprouts and zucchini are a great accompaniment. Plus, they're healthy!

2 tablespoons olive oil
1 pound chicken breasts
1 teaspoon chili powder
½ teaspoon garlic powder
½ teaspoon ground cayenne pepper
Salt
Freshly ground black pepper

1 pound Brussels sprouts, stemmed and quartered
1 pound zucchini, cut into ½-inch chunks
1 thyme sprig, leaves chopped
1 dill sprig, chopped
2 teaspoons unsalted butter

1. Preheat the oven to 375°F.
2. In a large, oven-safe pan over medium-high heat, pour in the olive oil. Season the chicken breasts with the chili powder, garlic powder, cayenne, salt, and pepper and add to the pan carefully once the oil is almost smoking.
3. Cook the chicken for 2 minutes per side, until the outsides are blackened but you can smell the spices. Add the Brussels sprouts and zucchini to the pan and sprinkle the thyme and dill over top, covering the chicken and the vegetables. Season the veggies with salt and pepper, if desired.
4. Bake for 12 minutes. Take the pan out, add the butter, and return to the oven for another 5 minutes, until the vegetables are brightly colored and the chicken is cooked to 165°F.
5. Let cool and transfer to 4 airtight containers. Store for 4 to 5 days in the refrigerator or up to 1 month in the freezer.

Per serving: Calories: 272; Fat: 11g; Protein: 30g; Carbohydrates: 14g; Fiber: 6g

Vegan Bolognese over Rigatoni Noodles

Makes 4 servings | Prep Time: 10 minutes | Cook Time: 25 minutes

Pasta is great for inexpensive meal prep. I especially enjoy hearty pastas loaded with lots of vegetables and covered in a sweet, tangy tomato sauce. Bolognese is usually made with a meaty tomato sauce, but this version is vegan. Instead of ground meat, I use lots of mushrooms and onions. It's a simple dish that keeps well in the refrigerator and freezer.

2 tablespoons olive oil
20 white button mushrooms, chopped
¼ cup chopped white onion
3 garlic cloves, finely chopped
3 cups plain tomato sauce
¼ cup water

2 teaspoons Italian seasoning
½ teaspoon red pepper flakes
7 ounces rigatoni noodles
Salt
Freshly ground black pepper

1. In a large pot over medium heat, pour in the olive oil. Add the mushrooms, onions, and garlic, and sauté for 5 to 6 minutes. The vegetables should be nicely caramelized and cooked down.
2. Pour in the tomato sauce and water and mix well. Add the Italian seasoning and red pepper flakes and bring to a simmer. Cover and cook for 15 to 20 minutes.
3. Meanwhile, bring a medium pot of salted water to a boil and cook the rigatoni according to package instructions. Once done, drain, cool, and portion into 4 airtight containers.
4. Add more salt and pepper to the Bolognese, if needed, and portion on top of the noodles. Let cool. Store 4 to 5 days in the refrigerator or up to 1 month in the freezer.

SMART SHOPPING: For recipes like this, look for larger cans of tomato sauce, which will usually be cheaper by volume.

Per serving: Calories: 315; Fat: 8g; Protein: 12g; Carbohydrates: 51g; Fiber: 6g

$1.75 PER PORTION

Sweet and Spicy Beef Lettuce Cups

Makes 4 servings | Prep Time: 5 minutes | Cook Time: 15 minutes

This recipe is one of my favorites. I've made these cups countless times for my wife, who loves them, and they are the perfect quick and easy meal. The crunch of iceberg lettuce goes well with the spice and tang of the ginger and hoisin sauce on the sautéed beef. If you don't have hoisin sauce, use 1 tablespoon of soy sauce and 1 tablespoon of honey or brown sugar. The recipe uses ground beef, frozen veggies, fresh mushrooms, and lots of garlic for a mouthwatering meal that will impress your friends and family.

1 tablespoon olive oil
1 pound lean ground beef
8 white button mushrooms, sliced
1 cup frozen bell peppers
½ cup sliced white onion
3 garlic cloves, finely chopped

1 teaspoon grated fresh ginger
2 tablespoons hoisin sauce
1 tablespoon water
½ head iceberg lettuce leaves,
    separated into cups

1. In a large pan over medium-high heat, pour in the olive oil. Add the beef and sauté, breaking it up, until it's browned, about 7 minutes.
2. Add the mushrooms, bell peppers, onion, garlic, and ginger and sauté for another 2 to 3 minutes, or until the vegetables are well caramelized.
3. Add the hoisin sauce and water and let the sauce come to a slight simmer. Don't over-reduce the hoisin because the dish can become too salty.
4. Portion into 4 airtight containers and let cool. Store the beef mixture separately from the lettuce cups. You can reheat the mixture in the microwave easily and then serve in the lettuce cups. Store for 4 to 5 days in the refrigerator or freeze the beef for up to 1 month.

SWAP TO SAVE: This dish works with ground pork or ground chicken as well, so feel free to switch it out since they are all cost-effective options.

Per serving: Calories: 232; Fat: 10g; Protein: 27g; Carbohydrates: 11g; Fiber: 2g

French Onion and Beef Soup

Makes 4 servings | Prep Time: 10 minutes | Cook Time: 1 hour

On a cold winter day, there is nothing better than a bowl of French onion soup—the caramelized onions, rich beef broth, and a cheesy crouton on top make for a satisfying meal. This version includes some delicious beef simmered for a long time to tenderize it. This allows you to use cheaper cuts, making this perfect for meal prep on a budget.

1 tablespoon olive oil
12 ounces beef top round, cut into
    ½-inch chunks
3 cups thinly sliced white onion
4 garlic cloves, finely chopped
4 cups beef stock

1 thyme sprig
1 tablespoon Dijon mustard
Salt
Freshly ground black pepper
2 leftover French bread slices
½ cup grated cheese of your choice

1. In a large pot over medium-high heat, pour in the olive oil. Add the beef and sear for about 5 minutes on all sides. Reduce the heat to medium, then add the onion and garlic, and cook for 10 to 15 minutes, stirring often, until golden brown.
2. Add the beef stock and thyme and bring it to a simmer. Cook for 45 minutes to an hour, until the beef is tender and falls apart. Stir in the mustard and season with salt and pepper.
3. Toast the leftover bread and tear into chunks. Store the bread and cheese separately from the soup in 4 airtight containers. When ready to serve, before heating, add the dry toast chunks to the soup and put the cheese on top to melt. This soup will last 4 to 5 days in the refrigerator or up to 1 month in the freezer.

SMART SHOPPING: Any cheap cuts of beef work well for this dish. I prefer cuts from the round, but you can also buy cheap cuts from the shoulder, such as flat iron or chuck steak.

Per serving: Calories: 298; Fat: 16g; Protein: 24g; Carbohydrates: 14g; Fiber: 2g

Chickpea Curry Rice Bowls

$2.65 PER PORTION

Makes 4 servings | Prep Time: 5 minutes | Cook Time: 20 minutes

These chickpea curry rice bowls are very simple to make, are packed with protein from the chickpeas, and have a flavorful coconut-based broth. The rice and chickpeas make this a very hearty dish.

1½ cups water
¾ cup medium-grain white rice
2 tablespoons olive oil
2 cups frozen vegetables (such as corn, carrots, peas, beans)
8 cremini mushrooms, quartered
¼ cup diced white onion
2 garlic cloves, finely chopped

¼-inch piece ginger, grated
2 teaspoons curry powder
1 cup full-fat coconut milk
¾ cup canned chickpeas, drained
1 tablespoon honey
Salt
Freshly ground black pepper

1. In a medium pot, combine the water and rice over medium heat. Bring it to a simmer, reduce the heat to low, cover, and cook for 20 to 25 minutes, until the water evaporates and the rice is nice and fluffy.
2. In a medium pot over medium heat, pour in the olive oil, then add the frozen vegetables, mushrooms, onion, garlic, and ginger. Cook for 3 to 4 minutes, until all the vegetables are caramelized.
3. Add the curry powder and cook for 2 to 3 minutes.
4. Pour in the coconut milk and simmer for 10 minutes, until the soup thickens.
5. Add the chickpeas and honey and simmer for another 10 minutes, until the flavors meld. Season with salt and pepper, to taste.
6. Store the chickpea curry in 4 airtight containers with the rice in the refrigerator for 4 to 5 days or up to 1 month in the freezer.

SWAP TO SAVE: Any frozen vegetables will work with this curry. I'm a big fan of broccoli, cauliflower, and corn.

Per serving: Calories: 459; Fat: 21g; Protein: 10g; Carbohydrates: 58g; Fiber: 8g

Chicken and Rice–Stuffed Peppers

Makes 4 servings | **Prep Time: 10 minutes** | **Cook Time: 40 minutes**

Stuffed peppers are a simple and easy dish to prepare. You can fill your peppers with anything you like—including quinoa, beans, or other grains— but a popular option is rice. It's filling and fits perfectly into a pepper. My version is Italian-inspired with a simple tomato sauce, chicken thighs, and frozen bell peppers.

1½ cups water
¾ cup medium-grain white rice
Salt
2 green bell peppers, halved
2 tablespoons olive oil, divided
Freshly ground black pepper
12 ounces boneless, skinless chicken
    thighs, diced

1 cup frozen bell peppers
¼ cup diced white onion
1 teaspoon garlic powder
1 teaspoon Italian seasoning
2 cups plain tomato sauce
1 teaspoon balsamic vinegar

1. Preheat the oven to 375°F.
2. In a small pot, combine the water and rice and season with salt. Bring to a simmer, then reduce the heat to low, cover, and cook for 25 minutes, until the water has evaporated and the rice is nice and fluffy. Let cool.
3. Coat the peppers with 1 tablespoon of olive oil, sprinkle with salt and pepper, and place on a baking sheet. Roast for 10 to 12 minutes. Let cool.
4. In a medium pot over medium-high heat, pour in the remaining tablespoon of olive oil. Brown the chicken for about 4 minutes. Add the frozen bell peppers, onion, garlic powder, and Italian seasoning and cook for 1 minute.
5. Pour in the tomato sauce and balsamic vinegar and simmer for 10 to 12 minutes, until the sauce thickens.
6. Add the rice, mix well, and stuff into the pepper halves. Store the stuffed peppers in 4 airtight containers for 4 to 5 days in the refrigerator or up to 1 month in the freezer.

SWAP TO SAVE: You can use pork, beef, or even seafood for these stuffed peppers.

Per serving: Calories: 349; Fat: 11g; Protein: 22g; Carbohydrates: 41g; Fiber: 4g

One-Pan Shrimp and Veggies

Makes 4 servings | Prep Time: 10 minutes | Cook Time: 20 minutes

One-pan meals are great for meal prep. It's simple to cook everything on the same baking sheet, and there are many ways to mix and match flavors and protein options. This version is a simple shrimp and vegetable meal, with mushrooms, peppers, onion, and zucchini, that is inexpensive, filling, and delicious. Try adding ½ cup frozen baby corn and 1 cup spinach for extra color and nutrition.

1 pound shrimp, peeled and deveined
1 large zucchini, sliced
2 cups frozen bell peppers
8 white button mushrooms, quartered
½ cup sliced white onion
2 tablespoons butter, melted

1 tablespoon olive oil
1 teaspoon garlic powder
1 teaspoon dried dill
1 teaspoon chili powder
Salt
Freshly ground black pepper

1. Preheat the oven to 375°F.
2. In a large bowl, combine the shrimp, zucchini, bell peppers, mushrooms, onion, butter, olive oil, garlic, dill, and chili powder. Season with salt and pepper.
3. Transfer to a large baking sheet and cook for 18 to 20 minutes, until the shrimp has turned pink and the vegetables are well caramelized.
4. Transfer to 4 airtight containers and store for 3 to 4 days in the refrigerator or up to 1 month in the freezer.

SWAP TO SAVE: Add whatever vegetables you like or have on hand for this dish.

Per serving: Calories: 206; Fat: 11g; Protein: 19g; Carbohydrates: 9g; Fiber: 2g

CHAPTER EIGHT

Snacks

Homemade Ranch Dip and Veggies

Makes 4 servings | Prep Time: 10 minutes

Vegetables dipped in creamy ranch dressing are a great snack. But store-bought dressings tend to be loaded with additives and processed ingredients. This simple recipe for a homemade ranch uses Greek yogurt, mayonnaise, and simple seasonings and is a close stand-in for store-bought options.

¾ cup plain, reduced-fat Greek yogurt
¼ cup mayonnaise
1 teaspoon garlic powder
1 teaspoon dried dill
Salt

Freshly ground black pepper
1 pound raw vegetables (such as
    carrots, celery, and bell peppers),
    for dipping

1. In a medium bowl, whisk the yogurt, mayonnaise, garlic powder, and dill. Season with salt and pepper.
2. Portion into 4 airtight containers, keeping the ranch and vegetables separate. Store in the refrigerator for 4 to 5 days.

SMART SHOPPING: The sky's the limit when it comes to the vegetables you can use for this dip. Go wild!

Per serving: Calories: 153; Fat: 11g; Protein: 5g; Carbohydrates: 10g; Fiber: 2g

Roasted Barbecue Chickpeas

Makes 4 servings | Prep Time: 5 minutes | Cook Time: 30 minutes

Roasted chickpeas are an easy snack to prepare. This is a great substitute for salty, store-bought snacks such as chips or pretzels. The chickpeas are roasted slowly in a low-temperature oven and left to dry out and become crunchy. My version is a simple barbecue flavor, but you might also enjoy dill pickle, or salt and vinegar chickpeas.

2 (15-ounce) cans chickpeas, drained
1 tablespoon olive oil
½ teaspoon ground cayenne pepper
1 teaspoon chili powder

1 teaspoon garlic powder
Salt
Freshly ground black pepper

1. Preheat the oven to 300°F.
2. In a large bowl, combine the chickpeas, olive oil, cayenne, chili powder, and garlic powder. Season with salt and pepper.
3. Transfer to a large baking sheet in a single layer.
4. Roast for 30 minutes, stirring often. When done, the chickpeas will be dry and crunchy. Divide into 4 portions and store in airtight containers on the counter for 1 week.

SMART SHOPPING: Get the larger cans of chickpeas if you want to make a bigger batch; it will be even cheaper.

Per serving: Calories: 192; Fat: 6g; Protein: 8g; Carbohydrates: 27g; Fiber: 8g

Mini Hard-Boiled Egg Sandwiches

Makes 8 sandwiches | Prep Time: 5 minutes | Cook Time: 10 minutes

This is a fun little snack that you can customize any way you like. Once you hard-boil the eggs and peel them, you slice them in half to make mini sandwiches. These snacks are high in protein, too, so they're a win all around. My version is a simple vegetarian option with some tangy Dijon mayo.

8 large eggs
Salt
Freshly ground black pepper
½ teaspoon garlic powder
1 cup shredded iceberg lettuce

1 Roma tomato, sliced
¼ cup sliced red onion
1 tablespoon mayonnaise
1 teaspoon Dijon mustard

1. Place the eggs in a large pot and fill with enough water to just cover them.
2. Bring to a boil. Once boiling, cook the eggs for 8 minutes. Then run the eggs under cold water, peel them, and slice each egg in half lengthwise.
3. Season the eggs with salt, pepper, and garlic powder and build the sandwiches by adding the lettuce, tomato, and onion to the bottom egg half.
4. Mix the mayo and mustard and spread on the top half of the egg. Put the halves together. Store 2 eggs each in 4 airtight containers for up to 3 to 4 days in the refrigerator. This snack doesn't freeze well.

SMART SHOPPING: You can go with any theme for these egg sandwiches. Use sautéed mushrooms and cheese, make your own BLTs, or even try smoked salmon!

Per serving (2 sandwiches): Calories: 179; Fat: 12g; Protein: 13g; Carbohydrates: 4g; Fiber: 1g

Roasted Dill Pumpkin Seeds

Makes 4 servings | Prep Time: 3 minutes | Cook Time: 20 minutes

Raw pumpkin seeds are a great protein source. You can roast them easily and add a variety of flavors. My version is a tangy dill pickle pumpkin seed. Just toss the seeds in some dill, vinegar, garlic powder, salt, and pepper, and you'll have a healthy, addictive snack that will rival any chip or processed salty snack you might be craving.

1½ cups raw pumpkin seeds
1 teaspoon dried dill
1 teaspoon white wine vinegar
1 teaspoon garlic powder

1 teaspoon olive oil
Salt
Freshly ground black pepper

1. Preheat the oven to 350°F.
2. In a medium bowl, mix the pumpkin seeds, dill, vinegar, garlic powder, and olive oil, and season with salt and pepper.
3. Transfer to a large baking sheet. Make sure to spread out the pumpkin seeds so there is no overlap.
4. Roast for 20 minutes. Alternatively, you can also sauté them on the stove in a large pan over high heat for about 5 minutes. The pumpkin seeds can burn if left in the pan for too long, so keep an eye on them.
5. As soon as the seeds are roasted, transfer them to 4 airtight containers and store at room temperature for up to 2 weeks.

SMART SHOPPING: Buying pumpkin seeds in bulk is the way to go for this recipe. Pre-packaged pumpkin seeds can be more expensive.

Per serving: Calories: 268; Fat: 23g; Protein: 13g; Carbohydrates: 7g; Fiber: 3g

Garlic Parmesan Kale Chips

Makes 4 servings | Prep Time: 10 minutes | Cook Time: 15 minutes

Kale is all the rage these days, and one of the tastiest things you can do with it is to make kale chips! It's easy, and kale absorbs flavors so well that there are many options to work with. Similar to potato chips, there are many flavors—barbecue, salt and vinegar, or cheese—and the options are endless. One of my favorite ways to make kale chips is this one, with grated Parmesan cheese and lots of garlic.

2 bunches kale
2 tablespoons grated Parmesan cheese
2 tablespoons olive oil, plus more for
    greasing

2 teaspoons garlic powder
1 teaspoon white wine vinegar
Salt
Freshly ground black pepper

1. Preheat the oven to 350°F. Grease 2 baking sheets with olive oil or line with parchment paper.
2. Tear the kale leaves into strips after removing the entire stem; this part doesn't roast as well.
3. In a large bowl, toss the kale, Parmesan, olive oil, garlic powder, and vinegar, then season with salt and pepper and mix. You won't need to season the kale too much since it absorbs salt easily and can become too salty.
4. Transfer to 2 baking sheets, spreading out the kale so it has plenty of room.
5. Roast for 8 minutes, then check the kale and remove any leaves that are already crunchy. Finish roasting the kale for another 5 to 6 minutes; it should be golden brown.
6. Let cool and transfer to 4 airtight containers. Store on the counter for 1 week.

SMART SHOPPING: Buying whole heads of kale is the best way to go. They are heartier and roast better than buying the pre-packaged kale mixes.

Per serving: Calories: 91; Fat: 8g; Protein: 2g; Carbohydrates: 4g; Fiber: 1g

Toasted Pita Chips and Homemade Hummus

. . . .

Makes 4 servings | Prep Time: 5 minutes | Cook Time: 10 minutes

Homemade hummus is always a great way to get in some healthy protein. Hummus is good with everything from fresh vegetables to pitas or wraps. It's also easy to make and will last in your refrigerator up to a week. This version is served with toasted pita chips.

4 (8-inch) pitas, cut into small triangles
3 tablespoons olive oil, divided
Salt
Freshly ground black pepper
2 (15-ounce) cans chickpeas, drained

Juice and zest of 1 lemon
2 tablespoons chopped fresh cilantro (optional)
1 tablespoon garlic powder
1 tablespoon hot sauce

1. Preheat the oven to 375°F.
2. In a large bowl, toss the pita chips in 1 tablespoon of olive oil and season with salt and pepper.
3. Transfer to a baking sheet in a single layer and bake for 8 to 10 minutes, until golden brown. Cool.
4. While the pita is baking, combine the chickpeas, lemon juice and zest, cilantro (if using), garlic powder, and hot sauce in a food processor and puree until smooth. You may need to add 1 to 2 tablespoons of water to make sure everything purees smoothly. Season with salt and pepper.
5. Store the hummus and pita chips separately in 4 airtight containers. Store the hummus in the refrigerator for up to 1 week, and the pita chips on the counter, also for 1 week.

SMART SHOPPING: If you want to try something different, buy store-bought roasted garlic and replace it with the garlic powder in this recipe. Just 1 tablespoon of roasted garlic will do the trick and definitely change the flavor.

Per serving: Calories: 429; Fat: 15g; Protein: 15g; Carbohydrates: 64g; Fiber: 12g

Simple Greek Salad

• •

Makes 4 servings | Prep Time: 10 minutes

Greek salad is a great afternoon snack for me. I love all the crunchy vegetables, tangy dressing, and the strong taste of the feta and olives. This salad can be inexpensive as well, even with these ingredients. It all comes down to portion size and how you add flavor.

1 cup diced cucumbers
1 cup diced Roma tomatoes
1 cup diced green bell peppers
½ cup halved Kalamata olives
½ cup crumbled feta cheese
2 tablespoons olive oil

2 tablespoons red wine vinegar
1 teaspoon garlic powder
1 teaspoon Italian seasoning
Salt
Freshly ground black pepper

1. In a large bowl, combine the cucumbers, tomatoes, bell peppers, olives, feta, olive oil, vinegar, garlic powder, and Italian seasoning. Season with salt and pepper.
2. This salad tastes best when left to marinate overnight. Store in 4 airtight containers in the refrigerator for 4 to 5 days.

PREP TIP: You may be able to find pre-cut vegetables for a Greek salad in the produce aisle of the grocery store.

Per serving: Calories: 149; Fat: 13g; Protein: 4g; Carbohydrates: 6g; Fiber: 2g

No-Bake Banana Energy Bites

Makes 8 bites | Prep Time: 15 minutes

Energy bites and protein balls have become very popular, and for good reason. They're portable, healthy, and easy to adapt to your personal tastes or protein preferences. You can add all kinds of healthy fruit and grains, much like granola bars. My version uses dates, ripe bananas, and rolled oats to make a filling snack that you can take anywhere. They can also be frozen and thawed whenever you need a mid-morning pick-me-up!

1 cup pitted Medjool dates
1 ripe banana
1 teaspoon honey
½ teaspoon vanilla extract
¾ cup rolled oats

¼ cup unsweetened dried
   coconut flakes
½ teaspoon ground cinnamon
Pinch salt

1. In a food processor, combine the dates, banana, honey, and vanilla and blend until a paste forms. You may need to scrape the sides with a spatula a couple of times.
2. Transfer to a mixing bowl and add the oats, coconut flakes, and cinnamon. Add a touch of salt to bring out the flavors of the banana and coconut.
3. Roll into 8 even balls and store in 4 airtight containers in the refrigerator for up to 1 week or up to 1 month in the freezer.

SMART SHOPPING: Dates can be bought in bulk and are very inexpensive.

Per serving (2 balls): Calories: 216; Fat: 3g; Protein: 4g; Carbohydrates: 47g; Fiber: 6g

Measurement Conversions

	US Standard	US Standard (ounces)	Metric (approximate)
VOLUME EQUIVALENTS (LIQUID)	2 tablespoons	1 fl. oz.	30 mL
	¼ cup	2 fl. oz.	60 mL
	½ cup	4 fl. oz.	120 mL
	1 cup	8 fl. oz.	240 mL
	1½ cups	12 fl. oz.	355 mL
	2 cups or 1 pint	16 fl. oz.	475 mL
	4 cups or 1 quart	32 fl. oz.	1 L
	1 gallon	128 fl. oz.	4 L
VOLUME EQUIVALENTS (DRY)	⅛ teaspoon		0.5 mL
	¼ teaspoon		1 mL
	½ teaspoon		2 mL
	¾ teaspoon		4 mL
	1 teaspoon		5 mL
	1 tablespoon		15 mL
	¼ cup		59 mL
	⅓ cup		79 mL
	½ cup		118 mL
	⅔ cup		156 mL
	¾ cup		177 mL
	1 cup		235 mL
	2 cups or 1 pint		475 mL
	3 cups		700 mL
	4 cups or 1 quart		1 L
	½ gallon		2 L
	1 gallon		4 L
WEIGHT EQUIVALENTS	½ ounce		15 g
	1 ounce		30 g
	2 ounces		60 g
	4 ounces		115 g
	8 ounces		225 g
	12 ounces		340 g
	16 ounces or 1 pound		455 g

	Fahrenheit (F)	Celsius (C) (approximate)
OVEN TEMPERATURES	250°F	120°C
	300°F	150°C
	325°F	180°C
	375°F	190°C
	400°F	200°C
	425°F	220°C
	450°F	230°C

Index

Acknowledgments

I would love to thank my beautiful wife Heather, who is my best friend. I want to thank my parents for always letting me do what I wanted in life and never stood in my way. And I also want to thank that lovely couple who told me as a 17-year-old that I had cooked them the best steak they had ever eaten. If it weren't for them, I may not have stayed cooking for as long as I have.

About the Author

MATT KEARNS is a classically trained chef who has been in the restaurant industry for 20 years. He currently lives in Calgary, Alberta, with his wife Heather, their 2-year-old son Henry and 9-month-old daughter Salinger, and three lovely cats.

Printed in the USA
CPSIA information can be obtained
at www.ICGtesting.com
CBHW081510260124
3539CB00010B/14

9 781648 767043